HOW YOU CAN
STOP SMOKING
...permanently

by Ernest Caldwell

Foreword by MELVIN POWERS

Published by
Melvin Powers
WILSHIRE BOOK COMPANY
12015 Sherman Road
No. Hollywood, California 91605
Telephone: (213) 875-1711

ISBN 0-87980-074-7

FOREWORD

What a complex age we live in! We have preventions for small-pox, plague, typhoid, and beriberi—but, we are overrun with ulcers, mental breakdowns, and heart disease. Our automobiles, vitamins, dishwashers, and beauty parlors have given us everything but grace-ful, healthy, and happy lives. With the finest foods in the world we gorge ourselves until obesity has become a major American problem. And, an even greater problem than obesity is our nation's poor physi-cal condition, in spite of labor-saving devices. Our airplanes and big cars rush us, not to relaxing fresh air and sunshine, but to smoke-filled restaurants and nightclubs. The vigor of good health, the happiness of clean minds, and the joys of creative living have all eluded us—apparently because we cannot cope with the complexities of our age.

Occasionally, you run across a book that cuts through man's shams and pretenses. This is such a book. It rings with Truth, and will sharply jolt you out of your little circle of nail-biting complacency. Simply stated, the author says that most American adults who smoke are missing the fun and pleasures of life, as well as rapidly killing themselves. He describes the poisonous chemicals in tobacco, and then, summarizes medical research on the relationship of smoking to lung cancer, heart disease, Buerger's and Reynaud's diseases, digestive disorders, and cancer of the "T" zone. Actually, nicotine and tars aggravate any physical flaw or mental anxiety you may have. They rob you of natural vitality, and shorten your life span.

Have you noticed that most people take up smoking as a socially acceptable awkwardness to cover up less acceptable awkwardnesses such as clumsy bodies and minds? Thus is exploded the "belief bubbles" of smoking such as:

THE BIG LIE	THE TRUTH
"Smoking helps you relax..."	(Smoking increases tension)
"You blow your troubles away in smoke..."	(Concentrating on any object out-side yourself does the trick; smoking definitely not required)
"Smoking passes the time..."	(Smoking stirs the adrenals, thus making time move slower)

"It helps you think..."

(It gives you headaches on occasion, it causes memory lapses, it tires you faster and makes you more nervous — great help when you're trying to think!)

"A cigarette is a companion when you're alone..."

(Mr. Caldwell writes: "When I gave up smoking, I adopted another companion to keep me company when I was alone. I became a friend to myself. No more sitting down and staring at a little tube of white paper stuffed with tobacco! Now I had 15 minutes to spend with myself!")

The last section, "How to Stop Smoking," is the heart and secret of this book. The freedoms gained when you quit smoking are vividly shown. Other prescriptions for stopping the tobacco habit are described, but rejected for good reasons. You are told how to quit smoking *forever* — exactly, systematically, and permanently. This truth is driven home again and again: "When you stop smoking you return to yourself, and find your own long lost zest and zeal for life."

Melvin Powers
Publisher

12015 Sherman Road
No. Hollywood, California 91605

Contents

Introducing a Cure Without Drugs

If you're curious about how smoking affects you, if you're worried about smoking too much—what it's doing to your health and your nerves—this book is for you. It will show you how to break the tobacco habit quickly, easily, almost painlessly.

Maybe you'd rather dispense with a book. How much easier to pop a pill into your mouth and let the drug do the job! Easier—if drugs were safe, if drugs did the job!

Before starting this book, I consulted several doctors and chemists in search of just such a drug. "Great idea!" said Dr. F——, puffing on a cigarette. "If there were such a drug available, you wouldn't find me smoking."

Some drugs, he explained, are unscrupulously peddled as tobacco cures. No reputable physician would recommend them. One drug (I deliberately withhold the name) induces nausea. It nauseates you when you smoke; it also nauseates you when you eat. It may cause violent vomiting. It is too dangerous for a patient to take on his own.

Other drugs, sometimes peddled as tobacco cures, desensitize the mouth; they are anaesthetics. Their purpose is to kill the taste of tobacco; however, they also kill the taste of all food. Do you smoke for the taste? During a heavy cold, you can't taste anything, but you probably go on smoking.

Even if these drugs could discourage smoking, temporarily, they would not break the habit for you. As soon as you stopped using the drug, you would go right back to smoking. The drugs affect your mouth only, but the craving for tobacco is in your whole body. More than that, the craving grows during a drug-enforced abstinence. As soon as you stop taking the drug, your need to smoke is stronger than before. Smoking is also part of your habit system. Taking a drug does not help you break the habit; substituting a different system of habits does.

The habit of smoking is not governed by your mouth; it is governed by your mind. It is your mind which must be conditioned against smoking. That is the reason for this book.

Take the word of someone who has been through the experience. It's easy to stop smoking, easier than you ever imagined. Just make yourself comfortable, and read on.

This is not the old-fashioned crank attack on tobacco and sin. I wouldn't have the nerve to write one, considering that I smoked for 28 years, and averaged more than two packs a day for the last 10 years. Smoking is not immoral: it is dangerous.

If you smoke heavily, you are probably worried about all the talk on smoking and cancer. You want to know what there is to it. You want to know anything else science has found out about the effects of tobacco. Perhaps by this time, the smoking habit has become obnoxious to you. You'd like to break it if you knew how. Or perhaps you've had doctor's orders "to break it or else . . ."

Whatever the case, you'll find what you are looking for in this book. The section dealing with the effects of tobacco on the body represents the most recent and best medical research available. It has been gathered from numerous sources and put in simple layman's language. As you read, your questions on smoking will be answered. You will find startling and authoritative information on exactly how dangerous smoking is.

The cure for the tobacco habit will be discussed in due time. Don't worry about it now! All I want to establish at this point is the *possibility*, only the *possibility*, of success.

Why it should be I don't know, but the majority of smokers are convinced they can't quit. They feel doomed to defeat! Ask around! Some will point to previous failures. Others are afraid to try, afraid the attempt will make them nervous wrecks.

All this is nonsense. Smoking is a habit. You are not born with habits, you learn them. Anything you learn, you can unlearn. Remember, nobody ever died for lack of tobacco. Other smokers have broken the tobacco habit—and so can you.

I speak from experience. In 28 years of smoking, I must have consumed more than a quarter of a million cigarettes. That's a frightening number! Like all heavy smokers, I inhaled. I couldn't go anywhere or do anything without a cigarette dangling from my lips. My eyes were inflamed. I suffered continuously from nasal drip and sore throat. I had long since stopped getting any pleasure out of smoking. And yet, I never seriously considered quitting. The reason was fear, fear that I would fail.

A few months ago, I stopped smoking! Not on my own account, at first, but out of consideration for a member of my family who was stricken with a heart attack. I was afraid that my smoking would make it harder for the patient to stop.

And so I quit! You will learn the method I used. It proved easy, easier than I had ever dreamed. Had I known beforehand how little trouble it would be, I would have done it years ago.

My experience has been corroborated by many other ex-smokers. That's why I say to you, with complete confidence, don't worry about your eventual success. Right now, I am asking you to believe, to take it for granted, that when you're ready to stop, you'll do it without trouble.

Don't worry about will power. You are not testing your will. You are concerned with a habit, formed almost without your realization, that can be broken. When you are truly convinced of the hazards of smoking, and the terrific nuisance it has become in your life, breaking the habit will be simple.

You can stop smoking!

The Medical Case Against Smoking

1. Watch Out! That Cigarette Is Loaded

Now that you've read the introduction, you are getting a little worried. Look at the pleasure I'll lose if I quit smoking, you say, coughing a little. I used to say the same thing myself, when I was a two-pack-a-day man, hating every cigarette I smoked.

But see what answer you get when you ask an ex-smoker if he'd like to go back to smoking. His emphatic "No!" will show you he enjoys pleasures you haven't found in your smoke-filled world.

Behind the blue curtain of smoke is the dictatorship of the cigarette. Dictatorships are created with propaganda and destroyed with truth. There is a battle proceeding now over smoking. Advertising propaganda booms out loudly, trying to drown the voices of the scientists.

Do the answers to the questions about smoking lie in advertising fancy or in scientific fact? What is in the smoke? Is there a safe way of smoking? Will you avoid the harmful effects of tobacco if you smoke a pipe or a cigar? Can smoking fewer cigarettes safeguard you from the damage that tobacco does to your system? These are the questions to be answered before examining the effects of smoking on your body.

ADVERTISING VERSUS SCIENCE

Cigarette ads say, naturally, that smoking is enjoyable. Beautiful girls, handsome men, famous people, stare at you from every ad. You fall into the habit of thinking about smoking in terms of the ads. You take your information about cigarettes from them. They say, "You'll get a lift from smoking." When you reach for a cigarette, you repeat to yourself, "I need a lift."

Suppose you read an advertisement which said that holding a loaded gun against your head and pulling the trigger, gives you a lift. Would you go out and buy a gun? On the surface, that's a silly question. You wouldn't do it because you know what would happen. The ads, however, tell you to buy cigarettes, and you buy them—just as I used to—without knowing the facts about smoking. You owe it to yourself to find out what happens every time you inhale a mouthful of smoke.

There *are* people who have spent their lives studying the effects of smoking upon human beings. They are doctors and scientists and medical research workers, experts in their fields, qualified to explain what happens when you smoke.

You have seen and heard the cigarette ads. You will now see what the experts have to say. You will find out why they declare smoking is bad for you. *You* are not equipped to make medical decisions; neither are the advertising copy writers, but the medical experts are. The scientists have discovered that smoking is harmful. They have found out that smoking aggravates certain diseases and causes others. As you learn what the leading authorities tell about smoking, you will see how far removed is advertising fancy from scientific fact.

WHAT'S IN THE SMOKE?

Every time you draw on a pipe or a cigar or a cigarette, you are exposed to a minimum of 45 different chemicals and poisons. Some laboratory workers say there may be as many as 200 separate elements in the smoke. Listed below are 22. These are among the most important elements and compounds found in the innocent-looking, soothing, blue smoke: lutidin, rubidin, formaldehyde, carbolic acid, methalymine, acreolin, collidine, viridin, arsenic, formic acid, nicotine, sulphide of hydrogen, pyrrol, furfurol, benzopyrene, methyl alcohol (wood alcohol), prussic acid (hydrocyanic acid), corodin, ammonia, methane, carbon monoxide, pyridine. Quite a mouthful for one puff of smoke! Everytime you smoke, all those chemicals invade your system.

What is known about them? Benzopyrene and lutidin come from tobacco tar. Mice develop cancer when exposed to tobacco tars. Biology laboratories use collidine for killing experimental animals. Collidine causes paralysis, and then death. Carbolic acid is one of the most powerful caustic (burning) poisons known. Prussic acid—a favorite of detective story writers—kills within minutes. Several states use prussic acid, in gaseous form, for the execution of criminals. Carbon monoxide, another killer, does its dirty work by preventing your blood from receiving sufficient oxygen. Methyl alcohol causes first blindness, then death.

Formaldehyde, another chemical in tobacco smoke, is used by morticians in embalming dead bodies. Arsenic, usually employed as a rat-killer, is another poison. In sufficient quantity, it is deadly to human beings. The Pure Food and Drug Laws of this country permit 1.43 parts per million of arsenic in our food. This tiny amount is the maximum considered safe for human beings. Tobacco has an arsenic content 50 times the amount legally permitted in food. While we do not eat cigarettes, tobacco smoke does carry the arsenic into the system.

NICOTINE—A NARCOTIC

Nicotine is also a grade-A poison and a narcotic. As much of a narcotic as opium or morphine! Like these other drugs, nicotine is also habit-forming. The body of the morphine addict gradually builds up a tolerance for the drug. He must use more and more morphine to get an effect. Nicotine, however, is unlike other drugs in this respect. The body never builds up any tolerance for it. As a matter of fact, the older you become, the greater the effect of nicotine upon your body. Your tolerance for nicotine decreases with age. Less nicotine can do more harm as you get older.

There are about 10.4 milligrams of nicotine per cigarette in the so-called denicotinized brands. In regular cigarettes, the average nicotine content per cigarette is 20.9 milligrams. Fifty milligrams, injected directly into the blood stream, can kill a human being as quickly as a bullet. Fifty milligrams of nicotine are the equivalent of three regular cigarettes or five denicotinized cigarettes.

Luckily, the body does not get the full nicotine content of a cigarette. From one cigarette, just about two milligrams of nicotine are absorbed by the system. Not enough to kill, but enough to damage the respiratory system, the circulatory system, and other parts of the body, as you shall see in the chapters that follow.

Consider what a single cigarette does to the heart beat. Smoking one cigarette adds as many as 28 more beats per minute to the work of the heart. This is an increase of almost 40%, and the heart is not intended to work at this rate of speed.

In that case, why aren't smokers dropping dead around us every day? A good question, but the answer may surprise you. Smokers *do* die every day. One cigarette or 10 certainly will not kill you, but continued smoking will do your body so much harm that you can shorten your life by as many as 10 years. The following chapters will give you the evidence.

IS THERE A 'SAFE' WAY OF SMOKING?

People who claim they don't inhale may feel safe from the harmful effects of smoking. What do the scientists say? Doctors have found that non-inhalers get at least two-thirds as much smoke into their systems as the smokers. The mucous membrane lining of the mouth, throat, and nose absorbs almost as much smoke as the mucous membrane lining of the lungs. Anyway, doctors have found that non-inhalers do inhale, accidentally, much oftener than they realize.

Furthermore, the saliva in your mouth dissolves nicotine, and does it quickly. The nicotine in the saliva is swallowed, traveling down the esophagus into the stomach. Your body is thus exposed, whether or not you inhale. There is no "safe" way of smoking. The contents of the smoke do get into your system.

YOU CAN'T BE HALF-SAFE—GIVE UP SMOKING TO BE SURE

Perhaps you still think there's an "out" for you. "I'm a moderate smoker," you say. Let's see how doctors classify smokers. Do you smoke 11 cigarettes a day? You are a heavy smoker. In all recent research on smoking, scientists have divided people into three groups. The first group includes all non-smokers; the second group, moderate smokers; the third group, listed as heavy smokers, takes in all who smoke 11 or more cigarettes a day.

A few cigarettes a day may not seem excessive, but it is the cumulative effect, day after day, which is so dangerous. Remember, your body never builds up a tolerance for nicotine.

It can never throw off the harmful effects of even small amounts of nicotine. What happens to a smoker's system, happens whether he consumes a few cigarettes a day or 40; the process is slower or faster—that's all. Cutting down is not enough; you cannot take half-measures.

2. Smoking Damages Your Lungs

Smoking causes lung cancer! This conclusion, based on years of painstaking research, recently broke like a bombshell on the unsuspecting public. Reports on the subject at a New York Dental Convention received widespread acclaim. The Minister of Health in Great Britain delivered a warning speech to Parliament. The best medical brains of this country and England agreed on the deadly connection between smoking and lung cancer.

You may ask what led medical researchers to associate smoking and cancer in the first place. Research workers, studying their charts, noted that lung cancer deaths had increased 400% in 20 years. They also noted that cigarette sales to the American public had jumped 400% in the same period. These figures didn't prove that smoking could cause cancer, but they indicated a clue worth investigating.

The second factor which caused scientists to look for a link between smoking and cancer was the nature of smoke. Smoke is an irritant, and cancer a disease caused by certain kinds of irritants. According to Dr. Alton Ochsner, past President of the American College of Surgeons, "No one can deny that smoking produces an irritation of the bronchial mucosa [lungs]. Irritation over a long period of time will produce changes in normal cells to make them grow wildly and produce cancer. It is indeed logical that an individual who . . . has a long continued irritation of the bronchial mucosa, as a result of smoking, is likely to develop cancer of the lung."

WHAT IS KNOWN ABOUT CANCER?

If smoking can cause cancer, why don't all smokers develop the disease? The answer is simple. Only certain people are susceptible to cancer. There is no known test, however, which can pick out these people in advance. There is absolutely no way of pre-determining whether you may develop a cancer. Taking a chance, by smoking, is like playing Russian Roulette, a game once favored by the aristocracy.

This game consists of loading one chamber of a revolver with a bullet. The chambers are then spun by hand. The gun is cocked and the player puts the nozzle to his head, his finger on the trigger. He has no way of knowing if the hammer is ready to fall on one of the empty chambers or the chamber which contains the bullet. He pulls the trigger, and sometimes he's lucky, sometimes not. You take the same chance of developing lung cancer when you smoke.

Although it is not known why cancer develops in some people and not in others, the method of development has often been observed. Cancer is a disease of the cells. Our bodies are made of millions of cells, divided into groups which perform various functions. One set of cells is muscle tissue, another nerve tissue, a third forms the lungs, a fourth the liver, etc. When cancer strikes one group of cells or another, the normal cells begin to grow at a dangerous rate. Then, these wildly multiplying cells develop into a malignant tumor in the area. From the tumor, the deadly cancerous cells spread to other parts of the body.

The cancerous cell development occurs in any part of the body that has been subject to irritation over an extended period of time. From the general practitioner to the cancer research expert, all doctors proclaim that smoke is irritating and harsh. Hospital records confirm the frequency with which heavy smokers develop cancer.

SMOKERS 20 TIMES MORE LIKELY TO DEVELOP LUNG CANCER THAN NON-SMOKERS

Research workers and scientists first checked hospital records of lung cancer patients. Doctors Ernest L. Wynder and Evarts Graham started with two groupings of hospital patients from all over the country. There were 684 lung cancer patients and 780 patients with other diseases.

The reason for picking two groups—one with lung cancers and one without—was to provide what scientists call a control or check. If the two groups resembled each other in everything but smoking, and if one group suffered from lung cancer and the other did not, then their smoking habits might provide a clue as to why one group had contracted lung cancer while the other had not. First, both groups were questioned in detail about their living habits to make sure that they were matched on the basis of age, income, and all other factors—except one. The initial questions asked nothing about smoking habits; that would come later.

THE EVIDENCE PILES UP

When the survey was completed, this is what the two physicians found: more than 98% of the cancer victims were smokers. Among the general hospital patients (without cancer) more than 80% did not smoke, or smoked only slightly. The majority of the cancer victims were heavy smokers. Less than one-fifth of the control group were heavy smokers.

This study, by Doctors Graham and Wynder, was only a first step. Next they began to compare the results of similar research by other scientists. In Great Britain, Doctor Doll and Doctor Hill, also cancer specialists, had made a report on the smoking habits of 2,930 patients. The conclusions of the British team were even more dramatic than those of their American colleagues. In studying twice as many people, the Englishmen found that people over 45 who smoke 25 or more cigarettes a day, run 50 times the risk of developing lung cancer that non-smokers do.

The two American experts proceeded to compile the results of other studies made in this country, the English study, and additional studies from Switzerland, Germany, Czechoslovakia, and Denmark. These studies included the records of 5,000 cancer patients, as well as control groups. Putting all the figures together, Dr. Wynder and Dr. Graham concluded that a person who smokes more than a pack a day, over a substantial period of time, is 20 times more likely to develop lung cancer than a non-smoker. It was this conclusion which was publicized at the New York Dental Convention mentioned at the beginning of the chapter.

The leaders in cancer research agreed that the Wynder-Graham study was the most complete of its kind, and they were in accord with its conclusions. Dr. Ochsner, at the same convention, corroborated the report from his own studies. Then he went on to explain what this data meant in terms of the future.

Dr. Ochsner said that the body of American physicians are "extremely concerned with the possibility that the male American population will be decimated [one out of every 10 will die] by cancer of the lung in another 50 years, if cigarette smoking increases as it has in the past. . . ." Since tobacco is known to have a definite connection with heart and circulatory diseases also, Dr. Ochsner continued by commenting unhappily, "Smoking may have the one virtue of killing its victims of heart disease, before they die of cancer."

TOBACCO TARS PROVED TO CAUSE CANCER

Since the statistical studies indicated that smoking is a causative factor in cancer, the scientists set about finding the exact cancer-causing agent in the smoke. Again, Dr. Graham and Dr. Wynder were in the forefront. Donning white coats, they left their statistical charts to enter the world of the laboratory.

The doctors knew, to begin with, that the smoker absorbs tobacco tars from the smoke. Dr. A. C. Ivy, of the University of Illinois, had spent many years investigating various aspects of smoking. He found that a person who smokes a pack of cigarettes a day, for 10 years, inhales 8 quarts of tar in that time.

Dr. Graham and Dr. Wynder decided to repeat an experiment with tobacco tars. They would paint the shaved backs of mice with a solution of tobacco tars. This same experiment had not produced conclusive results in the past, but the two doctors felt that previous researchers had not continued it for a long enough period. This time they would use stronger tobacco tar solutions, and they would use them oftener.

And so they set to work. Tar was removed from the smoke by a machine which smokes cigarettes as a human being would—except that the machine smokes 60 cigarettes at a time. The tar solution thus obtained was painted on the shaved backs of the mice, since the skin tissue in that area is similar to lung tissue.

There were 81 mice in the experiment. A weak solution of the tar was applied to each little rodent, three times a week. During the first two months they gradually tripled the strength of the solution. In the 42nd week, one mouse developed the first signs of cancer. It took about 72 weeks for cancer to develop in the average mouse.

Seventy-two weeks is about half the life span of a mouse. In human beings, it also takes about half a lifetime of smoking before lung cancer will develop. Half a human life span is approximately 30 to 35 years; lung cancer shows up after an individual has smoked for about 30 years, in most cases.

CONCLUSIONS OF MOUSE EXPERIMENT

The mouse experiment continued for about two years. At the end of this period, 44% of the mice had developed cancer. In previous experiments, the largest number of mice to develop cancer was 7%. Forty-four percent was a surprisingly high figure. The reason that all the mice did not develop cancer is that among mice, as among men, not all are cancer-susceptible.

Our team of researchers drew the following conclusions from their work: there is something in cigarette smoke which can produce a cancer. "This is no longer merely a possibility. Our experiments have proved it beyond a doubt."

This experiment, taken with all the other evidence, has convinced scientific groups throughout the world, of the truth of Dr. Graham's and Dr. Wynder's statement.

The tobacco industry has not been able to disprove the fact that smoking can cause cancer. The frantic campaign of the four billion dollar industry has fizzled. The rise in smoking and the increase of lung cancer fatalities tell a frightful story.

3. Smoking Damages Your Heart!

In this country, heart disease kills more people each year than any other cause. If you lose a kidney or a lung, you can still go on living fairly well; but if your heart stops functioning, you have no spare to fall back upon; and unfortunately smoking wreaks havoc on this one heart of yours!

NICOTINE PREVENTS PROPER BLOOD CIRCULATION

How the nicotine in the smoke hurts the heart and the circulatory system will be explained in these pages. Doctors call nicotine a vaso-constrictor. This simply means that nicotine causes the walls of the blood vessels to become smaller.

How did scientists arrive at this fact? They started by measuring tiny arteries (arterioles) in the retina of the eye, before and after smoking. The arterioles are easily seen and measured with the delicate instruments of the eye specialist. It was found that smoking narrowed the walls of the arterioles by 22%.

The Mayo Foundation conducted further research to verify these findings. Special medical photographers worked with very sensitive cameras to take pictures of blood vessels in the back of the eye. Lenses were trained on the tiny pupil of the eye; photographs were taken of these blood vessels, before and after smoking. The results were the same as in the previous experiment. After smoking one cigarette, the tiny blood vessels in the back of the eye narrowed 22%.

The experiments continued. Doctors know that when the arteries in an area are constricted, the body temperature drops. Thus they would find out whether smoking constricts blood vessels in the hands and feet. Two groups of doctors carried out separate but similar experiments to check the effect of nicotine on blood vessels in the body extremities.

At the University of Michigan, Drs. Maddock and Coller handed out cigarettes—one apiece—to the subjects in their test. They checked the hand temperature and foot temperature of each subject before he smoked. After he had finished smoking, they again checked temperatures. Almost invariably, they found that the temperature had dropped, sometimes 5.3 degrees Fahrenheit. The same thing happened at New York Post Graduate Hospital. Two physicians there, Wright and Moffat, followed the same procedure. The results of the test they made were the same as the Michigan test.

The doctors also noted other manifestations of the effects of nicotine. Beneath the fingernails are very tiny blood vessels, and after smoking, these closed completely. The smaller the blood vessel, the more it was affected by the nicotine. The effect was greatest on peripheral blood vessels, they noted. Peripheral blood vessels are found in many parts of the body, in the hands and feet and eyes, where the doctors measured the constriction caused by nicotine. The heart also is composed of peripheral blood vessels—the whole heart wall. Thus, every time you smoke, the blood vessels in the heart are narrowed.

Another discovery in connection with the experiments was the demonstration of the speed with which nicotine works. After the first puff of a cigarette, the doctors found, the blood flow to the hands is cut in half. Further, it takes more than an hour for the rate of blood flow through peripheral vessels to return to normal. Think of what this means, if you smoke only one cigarette an hour. Your circulation is not normal, all day long, and your circulation does not return to normal until after you are in bed, asleep.

IMPAIRED CIRCULATION DAMAGES BODY

Why is proper circulation of the blood so important? Every inch of the body, every organ like the heart or the kidneys, must receive nourishment. Nourishment is carried in the blood. Every part must have oxygen, from the brain to the toes. Oxygen is also carried in the blood. Every set of muscles, every section of the body gives off waste products in doing its job; these wastes are taken away by the blood. Blood brings food and oxygen, and removes waste materials.

When an area of the body lacks proper circulation, it does not receive enough nourishment to do its work properly. It is also slowly poisoned by the accumulating wastes because there is not sufficient blood flowing to remove the wastes completely. Since nicotine constricts blood vessels in various parts of the body, the impaired circulation causes damage.

JUST ONE CIGARETTE MAY BE FATAL IN BUERGER'S DISEASE

A spectacular illustration of the effects of smoking occurs in Buerger's disease, a disturbance of the circulatory system which attacks men. Its counterpart in women is called Reynaud's disease. This disease occurs in the extremities, that is, the hands or the feet. Buerger's disease first affects one hand or one foot; Reynaud's disease, both arms.

Patients find that the afflicted area turns cold, then white. If the disease is not checked at this point, gangrene sets in, and unless the hand or foot is amputated, death follows. Why does this happen? Simply because the circulation to the affected area is greatly reduced or stops completely. Luckily, this is a fairly rare disease.

How does smoking figure in this? Buerger's disease is a circulatory disturbance, and smoking impairs circulation markedly. Further, there is no known sufferer from Buerger's disease (or Reynaud's disease) who is not a smoker.

Look at the record! In a study of 1,000 cases of Buerger's disease, all 1,000 were smokers. New York's Mt. Sinai Hospital checked 1,400 cases. In 1,400 cases—1,400 smokers! At the Mayo Clinic, Dr. Wayward T. Horton examined the records of 948 cases—all smokers. Dr. Samuels, studying this same condition, concluded that all patients with the disease were smokers.

Buerger's disease is actually a deadly allergy to tobacco. People so afflicted are extraordinarily sensitive to the effects of nicotine. (Remember, however, that what happens to them in the course of the disease also happens to the average smoker, in a much milder manner, of course.)

There is serious trouble when patients with Buerger's disease refuse to give up smoking. Lesions (open sores) will not heal as long as the patient continues to smoke. Even after apparent healing, the lesions reappear rapidly if the patient resumes his smoking. One cigarette can disrupt the healing process, the lesion appearing immediately as the patient smokes his first cigarette. In some cases, the smoking of one cigarette will even cause death.

There is one cheerful note in this picture. We find it in a report by Dr. Irving S. Wright. He describes the histories of 100 patients. Of them, 97 recovered successfully because they stopped smoking. Three cases worsened and had to undergo amputations; these 3 patients refused to heed the doctor's instructions to stop smoking.

Buerger's disease shows the effect of nicotine on the peripheral blood vessels in the hands and feet. Since the heart is nourished entirely by peripheral blood vessels, we can deduce what happens to the heart when you smoke. Even though most smokers will never develop Buerger's disease, and the somewhat narrowed blood vessels in hands and feet may not be too serious, it is another story with the constricted blood vessels in the heart.

HOW THE MOST IMPORTANT ORGAN IN YOUR BODY WORKS

Of all parts of the body, your heart is the most important. It is actually a big muscle. Opening and closing, it operates like a pump, sending the blood through the arteries to all portions of your body. This arterial blood, pumped by the heart, carries the food and oxygen needed for nourishment and life. As the blood goes out to every square inch of the body depositing its precious freight, so must it return, laden with waste materials. It returns through the veins, leaving the waste products it has picked up in the proper depositories. When the blood reaches the heart again, it has been purified. The veins and arteries are the pipes in this pumping system.

Your heart is the only organ in your body which works constantly. It must carry on the function just described day and night. Your liver and your kidneys rest every so often. Even your lungs get a rest when your breathing slows down at night and becomes more shallow. Your heart beats 24 hours a day. In one hour, the normal heart beats 4,500 times; 108,000 times a day; day in and day out it works like this. Each beat is a contraction of the heart muscle, sending the blood all over your body. Between each beat, your heart rests for less than half a second.

In order to carry on this work, the heart should get all the nourishment and oxygen it needs. The blood which passes through the heart does not do this job; there are special arteries to bring the needed food and air to the heart muscle. These are the coronary arteries. From the coronary artery, the blood passes into the small peripheral blood vessels of the heart muscle itself. All the vessels of the heart muscle are peripheral vessels; and it is the peripheral vessels which are so greatly affected by nicotine!

If smoking narrows the blood vessels of the heart as well as other sections of the body, the heart must work harder than normal. To send the same amount of blood through the constricted arteries, the heart must beat faster; therefore its already tiny intervals of rest are shortened. The heart muscle produces more waste products; but the narrowed vessels have less chance to carry those wastes away, just as they can bring less food and oxygen to the overworked heart.

The smoker's heart always has a faster beat than the normal heart. You can prove it to yourself with a simple experiment. The first thing in the morning, before you smoke, count your pulse beat. Then take your pulse beat again after your first cigarette. You will find it has jumped anywhere from 10 to 30 beats more per minute.

HEART DISEASE OCCURS SIX TIMES OFTENER AMONG SMOKERS

As far back as 1940, doctors had significant facts on the coronary death rate of smokers and non-smokers. At that time, the Mayo Foundation analyzed the work of Doctors English, Willius, and Berkson—leading heart specialists. They found that six times as many smokers died of coronary heart diseases as non-smokers.

Coronary heart disease is very often called "doctors' disease" because so many doctors die from it. The Journal of the American Medical Association studied the coronary death rate of doctors. In one year 3,460 physicians died; more than one-third of those deaths were due to coronary heart disease.

Another survey analyzed the heart attacks suffered by the doctors of the Dallas County Medical Society. In every case, the physician suffering from a heart attack was a steady user of tobacco, but there was not one single non-smoker, under the age of 60, who had suffered from a heart attack.

The question surely must arise in your mind, "Why do doctors smoke, if all these facts about smoking are so?" The average doctor smokes for the same reason you do. He is just as human as you or I. Very often he ignores medical facts about tobacco. He postpones examining these facts even though they are at his fingertips. He finds the same difficulties in giving up smoking and defends his failure with the same unscientific rationalizations as you or I.

This was made very clear to me when our family doctor told my wife that she must give up smoking because of her heart condition. As she walked out of the consulting room, he lit a cigarette. Watching this, I jumped on him, and he defended himself shamefacedly.

"I know I shouldn't smoke," said he, "but you know how it is. A doctor's on call 24 hours a day. It's a strain!"

"More of a strain than smoking?" I asked.

"Of course not," he admitted. "To tell the truth, smoking makes it worse. But it's so hard to quit."

That wasn't the end of the story, however. When his own medical check-up revealed a heart condition, he stopped like a shot.

Some months later, he was telling me how much better he was feeling. He added, "Sometimes, I think we doctors are the worst patients of all. I should have stopped smoking years ago. It's the old story of, 'Do as I say, not as I do.'"

TOBACCO HEART

Dr. Harry Golston, another leading heart specialist, has done much research on the relation between smoking and heart disease. In an article in the Virginia Medical Monthly, he explains why the smoker's mistreated heart so often succumbs to disease. The "tobacco heart," he explains, is manifested by a pain in the heart or stomach area. It can be either a short, stabbing pain or a dull, constant soreness. It occurs often at night, when the individual is in bed. Doctors call this a functional condition. That means the pain and impairment of the heart will vanish when the smoking stops— if it stops soon enough. Dr. Golston continues by saying that this temporary impairment can turn into a permanent disability if you continue to smoke!

There is another type of heart disease called angina pectoris. One of the symptoms of angina is excruciating, sharp pains in the chest. Dr. Hubert Blanc says that death may very well result from the smoking of a single cigarette in some angina patients.

HEART ATTACK

In the case of coronary thrombosis, or coronary occlusion, death results when the coronary artery is completely blocked or "occluded." When a smaller section of the heart is cut off from circulation, the heart attack is not necessarily fatal. Given time and rest, the heart develops new networks of blood vessels to take the place of those cut off. Heart attacks do not occur in normal heart arteries—only in those that have already been narrowed over a period of time.

The progress of heart disease cannot be watched like Buerger's disease; but examination of smokers' hearts after death shows the same damage to tissue that is present in Buerger's disease. As just one of many studies, we note the report by Dr. H. Brooks in the New York Journal of Medicine. Dr. Brooks performed autopsies on 54 smokers in order to examine their hearts. There was degeneration of tissue in every one. The damage was the kind which results from an insufficient blood supply.

No one need tell you that heart disease is serious, especially when you have seen that it is the biggest killer today. Perhaps you don't know that the death rate from heart disease, like the rate of smoking, has been rising steadily each year. Once heart disease has attacked an individual, he is usually forbidden to smoke. Why risk your life, why wait until heart trouble develops, before you stop?

SMOKING CAN KILL IN CIRCULATORY DISEASES

You have already observed what smoking can do in Buerger's or Reynaud's disease. Now you will see some of the more common circulatory diseases, like hypertension (high blood pressure) and arteriosclerosis (hardening of the arteries).

Dr. Grace M. Roth, of the Mayo Clinic, is one of the leading research workers in heart and circulatory diseases. In a recent report she stated that smoking or not smoking can mean the difference between life and death in diseases of the circulation and the heart.

To see why this is so, note what happens to the blood pressure when you smoke. Smoking increases the blood pressure (which, for the average healthy adult is 120 systoles). Mayo Clinic tests showed that smoking raises everybody's blood pressure. However, it raises the blood pressure of people suffering from hypertension even more than it raises the blood pressure of other people. In a test, 30 people with normal blood pressure showed an average rise of 21 after smoking two cigarettes. Fifty-six people with high blood pressure showed a rise of 31 systoles. And these were people whose blood pressure was already much too high!

Even more significant was the difference in the blood pressure rise between smokers and non-smokers. The blood pressure of non-smokers only rose an average of 26 systoles, but the blood pressure of smokers rose way above their usual norm, 40 systoles more than their normal pressure.

Here is further proof of a fact mentioned earlier, your body never develops a tolerance for tobacco; on the contrary, the tolerance decreases as you continue to smoke. That was why the blood pressure of smokers rose more than the blood pressure of non-smokers—after smoking two cigarettes for this experiment. The nicotine affected the smokers more, because they had less tolerance than the non-smokers. The habitual smoker's blood pressure is one-third above normal.

SMOKING AND ARTERIOSCLEROSIS

In arteriosclerosis, or hardening of the arteries, the walls of the blood vessels are narrowed by the disease. Nicotine constricts these already narrow walls still more. No wonder Dr. Roth said smoking can mean the difference between life and death.

To all the tests described in this chapter, there is another fact we must add. Smoking so-called denicotinized cigarettes produces the same results we have described. Cigarettes containing half as much nicotine as the average brand have exactly the same effect on the heart and the circulatory system as regular cigarettes.

4. Smoking Damages Your Digestive System

People have always recognized that the digestive system, especially the stomach, is a very sensitive part of the body. The Greeks used to call the stomach the seat of the emotions. In old England, people would complain about things that bothered them by saying, "It goes against my stomach." Today, we name our times, "the ulcer age." In a way, we're lucky the digestive system is such a sensitive mechanism, because we find out sooner when something goes wrong. The damage smoking does to the heart and lungs, for example, may not show up until it is too late. The digestive system protests right away when it is being misused.

Continued abuse of the digestive system can lead to ulcers. But first, take a look at one significant example. This is what happened to a group of 26 ulcer patients whom Dr. Irving Ehrenfeld observed for a year. They stopped smoking altogether when their treatment for ulcers started and improved without exception. All responded favorably to treatment. Afterwards, 11 returned to smoking. Every one of the 11 immediately developed the disease again. Their ulcers reappeared.

DOCTORS FORBID ULCER PATIENTS TO SMOKE

Dr. Ivy, one of the foremost researchers on the effects of tobacco, condemns smoking in an article for the American Medical Association Journal. He describes the findings of a series of experiments concerning the effects of smoking on the alimentary tract (the digestive system). Smoking is harmful to the ulcer sufferer, he maintains. He goes on to say that even the healthy person (without ulcers) should avoid smoking because of its damage to the digestive system.

Another leading authority, Dr. Alton Ochsner, whom we have met through his work on cancer, refuses to treat patients at his New Orleans Clinic unless they agree to give up smoking. It is impossible to cure peptic ulcers while the patient smokes, he insists.

SMOKING CREATES OVER-ACID CONDITION IN STOMACH

As in heart disease, nicotine is again the villain, preventing the ulcer patient who smokes from recovering. Nicotine creates a condition of hyperacidity in the stomach; this is harmful to the average person and downright dangerous to the ulcer sufferer, for ulcers thrive in such surroundings.

To protect the stomach wall from the strong acid digestive juices stands a thin lining of cells. These cells lie between the stomach wall and the food which is being digested in the stomach. If the protective lining were not there, the gastric juices would eat at the wall of the stomach instead of digesting (breaking down) the food in the stomach. This protective lining of cells is sufficient for the normal, healthy stomach. If the stomach produces too much acid, the protective cells no longer protect the stomach wall.

When you smoke, the nicotine constricts and irritates the terminal vessels in the stomach wall and the protective lining. The irritation makes your stomach manufacture an excess of acids.

If you smoke to quiet hunger pangs, you are creating an over-acid condition in your stomach. When you are hungry, your stomach normally starts to contract every so often. This is the stomach's way of notifying you that your body should have some food. Smoking a cigarette stops the hunger pangs because the nicotine acts on stomach nerves. The contractions of the stomach cease. In an empty stomach which is still and idle, acid secretions accumulate, often causing gas or heartburn. Heartburn's unpleasant, sour taste comes from the backing up of digestive juices into your throat.

Recurrent indigestion and stomach spasms can be caused by smoking. Such disturbances are also symptoms of hyperacidity; and they interfere with proper nourishment. Even with an excellent diet, your body is robbed of many food values when you are plagued by continual digestive upsets.

And so you see that heartburn, gas, a gnawing sensation in the solar plexus, and recurrent indigestion can be caused by smoking. Irritation of terminal vessels in the stomach by nicotine makes the stomach produce too much of the strong acid digestive juices. In turn, this hyperacidity causes the unpleasant symptoms described above. Any time the stomach produces more acids than necessary for digestion, the condition favors growth of an ulcer.

SMOKING CAN CAUSE ULCERS

Dr. Bole, gastro-intestinal specialist, states unequivocally that the action of nicotine upon the terminal blood vessels of the stomach causes ulcers. In this disease, the stomach actually devours itself as the ulcer develops!

Nicotine not only irritates the stomach wall; it also slows down the action of the protective cells lining the stomach wall. (It is the mucus those cells secrete which prevents the acid digestive juices from getting at the stomach wall.) This is easy to see. Think of how hot and dry your mouth becomes after you have been smoking for a while. Like the inside of your stomach, your mouth is also lined with mucous cells. What happens in your mouth when you smoke, also happens in your stomach: the secretions dry up.

The over-supply of digestive acids in a smoker's stomach, and the slowing down of the secretions protecting the stomach wall, can cause a sore or lesion to develop. This happens because the acid can not get at the stomach wall. Constantly bathed by acid gastric juices, the lesion does not heal. The unhappy smoker has become an ulcer patient.

The treatment of ulcers consists in reducing the hyperacidity of the stomach. The ulcer patient is forbidden to smoke. He loses many pleasures of eating because his diet is greatly restricted. He is forbidden to drink. He is told to avoid situations which make him tense and nervous.

SMOKING AGGRAVATES ULCERS

Tense, emotional people can save themselves much grief if they avoid smoking. This habit, to which so many are addicted, neither helps their nervousness nor relieves their tension. And it very often leads them to develop an ulcer condition which they could otherwise have avoided.

What about jittery people, those who cry, "I'll go crazy if I don't get a cigarette"? Will the cigarette calm them down, thus helping avoid ulcers? Not at all! Smoking doesn't soothe the nerves; it irritates them. (You'll see why later.) Taking a cigarette is the worst thing to do when you feel nervous. It will make you tenser and further stimulate the acid activity of your stomach.

Like all diseases connected with smoking, ulcers are on the upsurge. During the war, for example, more soldiers in the Canadian Army suffered from peptic ulcers than any other illness. The editor of the Canadian Medical Journal attributed the high incidence of ulcers to the combination of strain and smoking. Dr. Boles, writing for our American Medical Association Journal, makes the same observation of our American soldiers.

All leading authorities are agreed that smoking not only aggravates already-developed ulcers but also can cause the development of ulcers. In addition, smoking has a bad effect on other parts of the digestive system.

SMOKING INJURES THE LIVER

The liver has two jobs—it aids in the digestive process, and it acts as the body's watchdog. The liver removes organic poisons from the blood. For example, morphine is an organic poison; it is also a pain-killer. Morphine is sometimes given under medical supervision to deaden pain and bring rest to a patient. The liver removes enough of the morphine from your blood so that it will not harm you. What remains in your body is sufficient to relieve the pain. Without the action of the liver, the morphine would kill you. As with all dangerous, poisonous drugs, morphine is given only under the direct supervision of a physician. That is, all dangerous poisons—except nicotine!

For smokers, the liver must work overtime, constantly removing as much of the poisonous nicotine as possible. The liver cannot succeed in removing all of it. Much remains in the body, according to leading specialists. The presence of nicotine in the liver, plus the work in removing even part of the nicotine, puts too much strain on this hard working organ.

There is another substance in the smoke which the liver must act to remove. This is arsenic, also a poison. A tiny amount of arsenic is allowable, according to law. As you have seen, there is 50 times as much arsenic in tobacco as the Pure Food and Drug Act considers safe in food. This arsenic invades your body in the smoke. The liver can easily remove the tiny amount found in some foods. It has to work harder to remove the much greater amount of arsenic in the smoke. The liver can't always do it. That is why you have reports of arsenic poisoning among smokers.

The presence of nicotine and arsenic in the smoke makes the liver overwork. An overworked liver will not perform its normal duties as well as it should. It will be more likely to break down under conditions of special strain. Smoking certainly cannot be good for your liver.

Tobacco, that "pleasant, soothing weed," is far from soothing to your digestive system. It causes chronic indigestion, heartburn, gas, and stomach spasms. Nicotine creates an over-acid condition in the stomach. That is why doctors forbid cigarettes to ulcer patients. Further, the over-acid stomach of the smoker provides the perfect breeding ground for ulcers; and smoking can cause ulcers. Smoking is also harmful for the liver.

The first, nasty-tasting cigarette before breakfast, the deadening after-dinner cigar, and all the smokes in between, are equally guilty in damaging your digestive system. Stomach trouble is unpleasant; ulcers are painful. When are you going to find out how pleasant life can be if you don't smoke?

5. Smoke Is Not Kind to Your T-Zone

Stop and think for a minute—how does your throat feel right now? Probably the way mine used to in the days I was smoking. If you're drawing on a cigarette, the smoke goes down your gullet harshly. There's usually phlegm collecting in your throat that you want to cough up. Your eyes feel somewhat irritated, your mouth is hot and rather dry. Maybe you're not smoking at this moment. Still, your throat is raw and raspy, as if someone went at it with a grater.

The heat generated by smoking is bad for your mouth and throat. It is an added irritant to cancer-susceptible people. You will see how smoking can cause cancer of the mouth, tongue, larynx, pharynx, palate, and other areas of the T-Zone. You will also see how another form of tobacco can cause cancer of the mouth—chewing tobacco. As a further proof of smoke's unkind effect upon your T-Zone, you will find that smokers are less resistant to coughs, colds, bronchitis, and other ailments of the respiratory tract.

Whatever the Madison Avenue advertising copy writers say about the mildness of cigarettes and the pleasures of smoking, the medical men contradict. The research scientists don't agree with advertising double-talk and gobbledygook.

SMOKING BLASTS YOUR T-ZONE WITH TOO MUCH HEAT

There is certainly no variation between brands of cigarettes in the temperature of the smoke you draw into your mouth. Mentholated cigarettes may seem "cool," but the temperature of the smoke is the same as the non-mentholated brands. The sensation of coolness is created by another irritant, menthol.

Every time you puff a cigarette, pipe, or cigar, you are drawing in a blast of smoke, with all its irritating chemicals, tar compounds, and high temperatures. Down your throat it goes, and into your lungs. As the smoke enters your mouth, its temperature can exceed 190 degrees Fahrenheit. That's almost the boiling point of water. I'm sure you've burned your tongue on a very hot mouthful of soup, at one time or other, and the soup wasn't boiling. It certainly didn't feel good, did it? No wonder your mouth feels "like a motorman's glove" after you've done some heavy smoking.

You smoke at least 5 or 6 times a day; more likely, 30 or 40 times. The average cigarette lasts about 10 minutes. If you take a puff once a minute, you've puffed 10 times on that cigarette. Thus, in a 10-minute period, your T-Zone is subjected to too much heat once a minute. By the time you have smoked three-quarters of a cigarette, the temperature of your mouth and lips is estimated to have reached 140 degrees Fahrenheit. Is this being "kind" to your T-Zone?

SMOKING CAN CAUSE T-ZONE CANCERS

Heat is an irritant. As you have already seen, changes occur in normal cells when they are subjected to continued irritation over a period of time. In people susceptible to cancer, constant irritation of any sort can be very dangerous, leading to the development of cancer.

Another irritant, dangerous to cancer-susceptible people, is nicotine. Nicotine is always present in cigarettes. Take a look at the amount of nicotine in 13 leading brands: Lucky Strikes, Camels, Piedmont, Richmond Straight Cut, Players, Old Golds, Chesterfields, Fatimas, Marlboros, Omars, Murads, Philip Morris, and Pall Mall have between 14 and 28 milligrams of nicotine per cigarette. So-called denicotinized brands and filter tips give you between 8 and 12 milligrams of nicotine per cigarette.

As a matter of fact there is no manufacturer who can claim to have removed *all* the nicotine from his cigarettes. Yet this would be the *only* way to prevent the destructive and irritating effects of nicotine upon the T-Zone. Anyway, it wouldn't do any good to remove all the nicotine from a cigarette. No one could smoke a cigarette like that. It would taste more awful than you can imagine. You wouldn't want it either, since one of the main reasons you smoke is addiction to the narcotic, nicotine.

Dr. J. L. Meyers talks about nicotine in his study of cancer of the respiratory tract. He explains that mucous membranes of the respiratory tract are irritated by nicotine; then they are injured by the tobacco tars in the smoke. Again, those cancer-causing tobacco tars!

According to the records of the Metropolitan Life Insurance Company, the death rate from cancer of the respiratory tract is rising (like the lung cancer death rate). This fact is related to the increase in smoking discussed in a previous chapter.

Dr. Ochsner, cancer expert, also confirms that smoking can cause cancer of the lip, mouth, and tongue. In these areas, it is the smoking of pipes and cigars which is especially to blame.

CHEWING TOBACCO CAN CAUSE CANCER OF THE MOUTH

Chewing tobacco may not be as familiar as other tobacco products, but there are large sections in this country where many people chew "baccy" or snuff. Tobacco in these forms is another cancer-causing agent. It has been so indicted by the American Cancer Society after a 2-year study. The research project took place at the Minnesota Hospital Tumor Clinic.

Case histories were taken of all men over 50 who were suffering from cancer of the mouth. Each patient was asked, "Do you chew tobacco or snuff?"

Almost 65% of the mouth cancer patients in the clinic had chewed for 15 years or more—a frightening toll!

The research workers also found that there were many other tobacco-chewing patients who had been addicted to the habit for less than 15 years. In these patients they discovered sores and lesions of the mouth which could become cancerous if the chewing of tobacco were not stopped.

SMOKERS MUCH LESS RESISTANT TO RESPIRATORY AILMENTS

Besides being subject to the danger of cancer in the respiratory tract, smokers are much less resistant than non-smokers to other respiratory diseases. As a matter of fact, Dr. W. L. Mendenhall pointed out, in a series of Harvard University lectures, that smoking causes serious irritation of the throat, larynx, and bronchii (all part of the T-Zone). Coughs, bronchitis, and tonsilitis, he explained, can be caused by smoking.

Dr. R. G. Hutchinson is a specialist in diseases of the mouth and throat. In cases of Vincent's Angina (inflammation of the tonsils) the effect of smoking is very great; it does extreme damage to the mucous membranes.

Medical statisticians have come up with facts and figures showing the effect of smoking upon respiratory diseases. Three doctors from the Life Extension Institute examined medical histories of more than 2,000 people. They found that nose and throat irritation, as well as colds, were four times as frequent among smokers as among non-smokers. They also found that three times as many smokers, as non-smokers, were subject to a constant cough.

6. Smoking Is Bad for What Ails You

Tobacco is an enemy from which there is no escape—as long as you smoke. In one way or another, it attacks you. If it doesn't come in through the front door and kill you with heart disease or cancer, then, slowly and subversively, it prevents you from recovering from other diseases, or undermines your health.

SMOKING INJURES TUBERCULAR PATIENTS

Doctors are practically unanimous in condemning smoking for tubercular patients. Constant irritation of a diseased lung by smoke makes it much harder for the body to bring that lung back to normal. In advanced cases of tuberculosis, smoking can mean the difference between life and death, says Dr. Samuel Wright of St. Mary's Hospital in London.

Tuberculosis may attack other parts of the body, as well as the lungs. An article in the American Medical Association Journal states that smokers suffering from tuberculosis often face an additional complication—laryngeal involvement. (The larynx is the "voice box.") In another article, Dr. Emil Bogen, chest expert, goes even further. He writes that tubercular patients who smoke and have laryngeal complications recover rapidly as soon as they stop smoking.

SMOKING CAUSES ADDITIONAL COMPLICATIONS FOR DIABETICS

The arteries of diabetics are constricted by the nature of their disease. As seen in the chapter on the heart, smoking also constricts blood vessels. Smokers suffering from diabetes really give themselves a raw deal. By smoking, they narrow still further blood vessels which are already constricted by disease.

Injuries in diabetic patients often become gangrenous. Gangrene occurs when there is extremely bad circulation. That is why smoking is so dangerous for the diabetic. He doubles his chances of developing gangrene from an infection.

Besides gangrene, there is another serious risk for diabetics who smoke. The majority develop thrombosis obliterans, or Buerger's disease. Only a third of non-smoking diabetics develop this disease. These are the conclusions of two doctors, Leonard Weinroth and Joseph Hirzstein. They made a study of 301 diabetics at Mt. Sinai Hospital. (You will remember that Buerger's disease affects blood pressure and circulation in the body extremities. Among non-diabetic patients, only smokers contract Buerger's disease.) Of the patients studied, Drs. Hirzstein and Weinroth found that 58% of the diabetic smokers developed Buerger's disease as against 37% of the diabetic non-smokers.

The physicians stated that smoking was the factor which made the difference, beyond any shadow of a doubt.

OVER-ACTIVE THYROID AGGRAVATED BY SMOKING

Research workers have found that smoking harms people who suffer from over-active thyroid glands. These people are usually thin; they are tense, nervous, and very excitable. For them, smoking causes attacks of sweating or flushing, tremors, nervousness, and fatigue, says the German gland expert, Dr. Kulbs.

Dr. F. Schlum, a scientist of note, relates that smoking raises the metabolic rate of people with over-active thyroids. These people already have a basal metabolism (metabolic rate) which is too high for healthy living.

SMOKERS A POOR RISK FOR ABDOMINAL SURGERY

Are you thinking about undergoing an abdominal operation? Do you know that smoking can cause additional complications? After surgery that annoying, apparently unimportant smoker's cough is dangerous. Such a cough involves a spasmodic movement in the abdominal region. Certainly bad for tissues which have just been under the knife! And it's practically impossible to repress the cough.

Dr. V. J. Morton has written an article for the surgeon's magazine, *Lancet,* about smokers. He points out that the death rate in abdominal surgery is six times higher for smokers than it is for non-smokers.

SMOKING CONTRIBUTES TO CERTAIN TYPES OF DEAFNESS

Smoking must be reckoned with in certain types of deafness. Smoke gets into the Eustachian tubes which lead from the nose and ears to the throat. When the tubes are irritated, catarrhal deafness may occur. Dr. Wyatt Wingrave accuses the pyridin in smoke; he says it is a contributory cause of irritation in the Eustachian tubes.

There is another type of deafness which occurs when the sensitive nerve tissue of the middle ear is damaged. This tissue is affected by nicotine. In an address to the American Otological Society, Dr. H. Marshall Taylor said tobacco can menace hearing. He singled out young people for special mention. When they come from families with a medical history of loss of hearing, the vital tissue of the middle ear is a danger spot.

SMOKING SPOILS COMPLEXIONS AND CAUSES SKIN AILMENTS

What smoking does to the complexion will interest my women readers especially. Of course, it affects women and men equally. Smoking sallows the skin and makes it wrinkle.

As you have seen, time and again, smoking constricts blood vessels in all peripheral regions of the body. This includes the face and neck. Constricted blood vessels mean the skin tissues are deprived of nourishment, and the undernourished skin becomes sallow.

Wrinkles often mark the smoker's face at an earlier age than usual. Skin remains firm while there are fatty tissues underneath. When the fatty tissues are consumed in an unsuccessful attempt to absorb nicotine, the skin sags. All the creams and lotions in the world won't put youth back into your face, once it's gone.

Along with its effect upon the complexion, smoking can cause very unpleasant skin ailments. Eczema and rashes afflict smokers whose nicotine tolerance is unusually low. Dr. E. B. Hollis has found that many tobacco workers and buyers are also subject to eczema and rashes. Eczema is a very severe irritation of the skin where the affected area becomes scaly and is subject to an annoying itch.

Another type of eczema is caused by the arsenic in the tobacco. Dr. Moyers and Dr. Throne examined a large group of smokers suffering from this skin ailment. In 30% of the cases, arsenic caused the eczema.

The only cure for this trouble is to stop smoking. There is no way of raising tobacco without using arsenic sprays to kill the insects that attack the tobacco plants. Once the sprays are used, there is no way of removing the arsenic from the tobacco.

And so it goes! This chapter has shown you still more ways in which smoking makes living difficult and unpleasant.

7. Smoking Takes the Joy Out of Living

Suppose someone offered you a magic formula. By using it you could bowl 225 instead of 150, run for a bus without puffing, see better, remember more, concentrate harder, and sleep better. Wouldn't you take the formula? Well, you've got it. You can do all these things. The formula is in your hands this very moment.

Give up smoking and you can get a lot more satisfaction out of living. Smoking cuts down your endurance. It makes you nervous and increases tensions. It decreases your vision and lessens coordination. It slows your mental responses by interfering with memory and concentration. In this chapter you'll see just how smoking affects all these aspects of day-to-day living.

SMOKING CUTS DOWN YOUR ENDURANCE

Endurance makes you more efficient in everything you do. Long distance runners and swimmers are not the only people who need endurance. No matter what you do—sit at a desk, drive a truck, work on farm or factory—you need endurance. Smokers have less staying power than non-smokers; they tire faster. Tired people make more mistakes and have more accidents; they have less energy.

Any activity you perform calls for energy. Whether you paint a house, dig coal, run races, drive a cab, or push a pen, you need energy. To supply the energy, your heart works hard. If you work and smoke, your heart has to work harder still. Remember those constricted blood vessels? The body tissues don't get enough food and oxygen; the waste products are not removed fast enough. The smoker's heart carries an extra load. That's why smoking makes fatigue set in more quickly, cutting endurance and ability to work.

Usually you talk about smoking and complain that it "cuts down your wind." Climbing stairs, you puff. Running for a bus, you breathe hard. When this happens, you call it "getting winded." It's not lack of wind or breath that causes this feeling; it's your heart, sending you a signal that it's working too hard.

You may not feel short of breath if you're turning out piece work on the production line; but tests show that you will produce less if you smoke. You may not feel short-winded if you work all day at a typewriter; but experiments reveal that smokers make more mistakes. Even smokers doing heavy work may not notice lack of breath; but research demonstrates that non-smokers doing hard physical labor suffer much less from fatigue. No matter what you do, smoking cuts down your endurance.

SMOKING CREATES NERVOUSNESS AND TENSION

More people are misled about the so-called "soothing" quality of tobacco than about any other aspect of smoking. Here is what researcher Harold Dingman found: smokers suffer 76% more from nervousness than non-smokers.

Symptoms of tobacco nervousness are irritability, headache, sluggishness, and insomnia. You know how you feel when you are under a strain—and how you smoke one cigarette after another to relieve that feeling. It is not the strain which is making you feel so bad. Much of the jittery, tight, nerve-stretched tension comes from the cigarettes you have been smoking. They increase your nervousness.

Like all smokers I used to say there was nothing like a cigarette for relaxing. Now I realize how mistaken I was. Since I've stopped smoking, I'm not half as nervous. I don't get the jitters. I can go to sleep at night. I still worry about problems, but they don't turn me into a jumpy, irritable person at the drop of a match.

There are sound medical reasons why smoking makes you tenser instead of calming you. The impact of smoke upon your system is like the impact of certain actions of the adrenal glands. These two glands are triggered to put you into motion fast in moments of danger and stress.

Through the adrenals, your body is readied, tensed, and supercharged to act in a tremendous hurry—to fight or to run. The body is enabled to perform superhuman feats of strength —as in the case of the man who lifted a car from the body of his son so that the boy could be saved before he was crushed to death. If you got emergency jolts from the adrenals regularly, your body would wear out in no time.

The similarity between the effect of smoking and the jolt the adrenals give you is this: in part, the adrenals act by constricting the blood vessels and speeding the heart beat; smoking does this too, as you well know. The action of the adrenals makes for tremendous tension in your body, but it takes place rarely. Since smoking has the same effect, it causes tension, not just on rare occasions, but day after day. If you want to relax, sit back, stretch, and take a deep breath. Don't light up a cigarette!

SMOKING IMPAIRS YOUR VISION

If you smoke, you see approximately 22% less than the non-smoker. Eating carrots won't help your eyesight unless you stop smoking. The nicotine in smoke cuts down your vision.

Nicotine affects the nervous system directly. The momentary, deceptively soothing effect of smoking occurs because the nerve endings are paralyzed. There is a very serious type of blindness caused by nicotine—amblyopia or tobacco blindness. It happens to people who are extremely sensitive to the nicotine in smoke. The nerve endings in the eye become permanently paralyzed; the eye can perform its functions no longer. Net result—permanent blindness! Luckily, this disease does not develop often. However, it is the daily impairment of vision which concerns most of us, and that is bad enough.

As early as 1944, eye specialists reported on what smoking does to the vision of flyers, especially at night. Under *normal* conditions, the higher the plane, the less the flyer can see.

Smoking even three cigarettes cuts normal vision in half for night flying. Here is the report the doctors made to a meeting of the Aero Medical Association.

Inhaling the smoke from three cigarettes impairs the flyer's vision. After smoking, his vision (on the ground) is restricted to what it would be if he were flying at an altitude of 8,000 feet. If a flyer smokes when he is flying at 8,000 feet, then his vision is cut down to what he would see if he were flying at 16,000 feet. I'd rather fly with a pilot who didn't smoke!

The Mayo Clinic has also investigated the relationship between sight and smoking. They found that the eye responds much less than it should to light for half an hour, after smoking two cigarettes. The results were the same whether the smoke was inhaled or not.

It was the University of Vermont's series of tests which proved that habitual smokers see 22% less than non-smokers. Those tests also showed that the "field of imagery"—what you can see at a single glance—was cut down by more than one-tenth for smokers. This could mean the difference between life and death to a driver.

For all sports which require accuracy of aim or vision, smoking is a big handicap to the participants. In test after test, smokers scored less than non-smokers. Marksmanship calls for very excellent vision. The 27 leading pistol shots in the United States do not smoke at all.

Whether you are marksman or mailman, smoking affects your vision. Seeing less, your efficiency is impaired and also your enjoyment of life.

SMOKING SPOILS COORDINATION

Coordination is a combination of practice in a particular field, steady nerves, good vision, muscular skill, judgment, and quick thinking. Vision and coordination are closely related. What cuts one down will impair the other. The cigarette ads to the contrary, it is well known that athletes in training do not smoke. Besides reducing endurance for the athlete, smoking lessens his coordination.

The University of Wisconsin ran elaborate tests to discover the relationship between coordination and smoking. The non-smoker's coordination was 60% better than the smoker's, the smoker retained this 60% loss for more than an hour after smoking one cigarette.

Coordination can mean the difference between life and death. Arctic explorers live in expectation of sudden danger. They know how to value coordination. Two of the best and most famous explorers in the world, Robert Peary and Vilhjalmur Stefansson, never smoked themselves nor accepted men who smoke for their expeditions.

Coordination is important to everybody, not just explorers and athletes. There are emergencies in your life which call for quick thinking and good coordination. Day in and day out, the way you do your job, the enjoyment you receive from recreation, your safety on the road depend on your coordination.

SMOKING STUPEFIES THE BRAIN

Why does smoking play such a big role in mental efficiency? The explanation is not complicated. Your brain is composed of the same sort of nerve tissue as your eyes. We have seen how smoking can paralyze the nerves in your eye. The optic (eye) nerves are an extension of the brain. Therefore, scientists explain, the nicotine which can deaden or even paralyze the optic nerve, can also affect the brain.

Researchers, seeking the connection between smoking and mental responses, have come up with some startling facts. Although 75% of the students at Harvard University smoke, no smoker has ever stood at the head of his class for the last 50 years. At Antioch, 75% of the heavy smokers fail; but only 30% of the non-smokers. At Yale University, 95% of the honor-winning students have been non-smokers. Smoking certainly seems to interfere with mental efficiency.

Further corroboration comes from Dr. W. E. Dixon. He reports on the results of 2,000 experiments where the effect of smoking on mental responses was tested. In all cases, he says, smoking lowered the mental efficiency from 10% to 23%. The tests also showed that memory is affected by smoking. Dr. Dixon found you have 38 times a better chance of remembering things well if you don't smoke.

What smoker wouldn't like to concentrate harder and remember better than he does now? You can, if you stop smoking. That is the encouraging fact in all this dismal information. As soon as you stop smoking, your mental faculties improve.

The cigarette you smoke can be obviously dangerous, like a thief waving a loaded gun; or it can rob you stealthily like the concealed embezzler. If a thief holds you up at gun-point, you know you are being robbed. To the patient with heart disease, smoking is an obvious danger; he knows one cigarette can rob him of his life.

To the apparently healthy man, smoking does not suggest sudden and open danger. Suppose a thief embezzles money, a little at a time from the bank where your life savings are deposited. You have no idea you are losing all your money. It is stolen little by little. So is the average smoker robbed of pleasures and life itself, little by little, without his awareness.

8. You'll Live Longer If You Don't Smoke

The other day, a 10-year-old nephew of mine announced that he figured to live forever. When I disagreed with him, he protested, "Lookit, Unc, they practically got ships to fly to the moon, 'n flyin' saucers, 'n space suits, 'n everything. I betcha they invent somethin', or find a secret power on one of the planets . . ." After a few minutes, he decided he wasn't convincing me and returned to his science-fiction story in disgust.

As an adult, you realize you can't live forever. But do you know you are cutting your life, perhaps 10 or 15 years, because you smoke?

What are the facts? Life expectancy for the whole country was recently figured as 66, with variations between the sexes and between different income groups. Dr. Raymond Pearl produced the most complete study ever made of life expectancy of smokers. He found that smokers have a considerably shorter life span than non-smokers. He also discovered that the younger you are, the more chance that smoking will rob you of your life. Maybe you can't live forever, but you can live longer if you don't smoke.

AVERAGE LIFE EXPECTANCY IS 66 YEARS

It is from the Metropolitan Life Insurance Company's tables that we quote the average life expectancy in the country as 66 years; however, if you break the figures down further, this is what you discover:

White people have a greater life expectancy than colored, because there is less poverty among the white members of our population than among the Negro, Asian, and Indian. Bad economic conditions prevent adequate maintenance of health.

Among the total population, there is another variation in the life span. Women have a greater life expectancy than men. White males can expect to live to be 67; white females almost 73. Non-white males will average almost 60 years of life; non-white females, almost 64 years.

One factor that may partly account for the difference in life expectancy between the sexes is smoking. Men smoke much more than women, and they have been smoking longer. Fewer women smoke, and smoke less, when they do.

DR. PEARL MAKES AUTHORITATIVE STUDY ON SMOKERS' LIFE SPAN

Dr. Raymond Pearl of Johns Hopkins University declares that smoking significantly cuts down the number of years you may expect to live. His conclusion is based on a detailed study of the life span of 300,000 persons, a study which the medical and scientific world regards as a classic. It is the most extensive piece of research on longevity and smoking ever made. It included 100,000 non-smokers, 100,000 light smokers, and 100,000 heavy smokers.

SMOKERS DIE SOONER THAN NON-SMOKERS

Specifically, what do Dr. Pearl's figures show? At age 60, 66½% of the non-smokers he studied were still alive, almost 62% of the light smokers, and only 46% of the heavy smokers. In other words, the odds are 3 to 2 that you will die sooner if you're a heavy smoker.

Only when you hit the age of 70 do the figures level off. Even then, there is a difference between non-smokers and smokers in the number of deaths. The greater number of deaths is in the column of the smokers, as usual.

Dr. Pearl does admit that a very few smokers reach a ripe old age. He explains this by saying that the smoker who has reached the age of 70 has a body which is much better equipped than the average person's to throw off the effects of tobacco. The 70-year-old smoker is also unusually resistant to the ills that normally beset a human being. Such a person, however, is the exception, not the rule.

THE YOUNGER YOU ARE, THE MORE YOU LOSE BY SMOKING

The death rate in the younger age groups of smokers is most alarming! The younger you are, the more years of life you will lose by smoking, for life expectancy keeps rising. Twice as many smokers die at 30 as non-smokers.

At 30, the odds for living to a ripe old age are 2 to 1 in your favor if you don't smoke. At 40, the favorable odds are even bigger for the non-smoker. In the fortieth year, heavy smokers die almost $2\frac{1}{2}$ times as often as non-smokers.

The odds begin to level off a little for the 50-year-old age group. Now the difference in death rates between heavy smokers and non-smokers is a little less than 2 to 1.

For all age groups, however, except 30, moderate smokers also die in greater numbers than non-smokers.

You have seen the various ways in which tobacco may affect the body. Smoking can cause many diseases like blindness, deafness, ulcers, cancer, heart disease, etc. It is a complicating and weakening factor in other illnesses. It lowers the whole physical tone of the body so that resistance is less. Is it any wonder that you won't live as long if you smoke?

9. No Safety in Filter Tips and Similar Innovations

Advertisements for less irritating, irritant-free, and filter tip cigarettes are increasing. Every day, more ads pound away at the so-called health angle. They suggest this, that, or the other brand is "kind to your throat," or "milder" than other cigarettes, or "contains less irritants." Trying to make sense out of these ads is like trying to see what's on the other side of a smoke screen; you can't do it!

In this case, where there is "smoke screen" talk, there is fire. How can smoking one brand of cigarettes be safe, and smoking every other brand be dangerous, when there are no appreciable differences among brands? The manufacture of filter tips and denicotinized cigarettes is a tacit admission by the tobacco industry that something is wrong. Unfortunately, these special cigarettes can offer you no protection against the hazards of smoking.

Filters and filter tip cigarettes do not guard you against the harmful effects of tobacco. King-size cigarettes do not filter the tars and nicotine out of the smoke. "Cool," mentholated cigarettes are just as hot as the others. Denicotinized cigarettes contain nicotine. Claims of "mildness" have no meaning. Smoking any of the cigarettes just mentioned doesn't protect your health against dangerous chemicals, tars, and poisons in the smoke. All the damage that regular cigarettes do, these cigarettes do also.

FILTERS TAKE OUT TASTE, NOT TROUBLE

Tests performed by independent laboratories show that filters and filter tip cigarettes reduce the amount of nicotine in the smoke by 25% to 50%. Medical authorities say this reduction does not mean anything.

The amount of nicotine in any filtered cigarette does significant damage to your heart and circulatory system. It kills patients suffering from Buerger's disease just as efficiently as an unfiltered cigarette. This fact has been proved in experiments already cited. As little as 25% of the nicotine found in filtered cigarettes makes your heart beat too fast. This was established by Columbia University's Department of Medicine and other researchers.

Filtered and filter tip cigarettes trap some of the tobacco tars but much still gets through. Unless *all* the tar is removed, you are not protected against the cancer-causing agent in the smoke. Smoking any kind of cigarettes causes hyperacidity and stomach trouble. Ulcer patients do not recover as long as they continue to smoke, whether the cigarettes are regular or filtered. All cigarettes, including filtered brands, are irritating to the mouth, nose, throat, and sinuses.

The foregoing statements are based on laboratory tests. They are backed by the American Medical Association, researchers from the Institute of Industrial Medicine, leaders in the American Cancer Society, Dr. A. Ochsner, cancer expert, and Dr. Robert L. Levy, heart specialist, among others.

KING-SIZE CIGARETTES OFFER NO PROTECTION

It is sometimes claimed that king-size cigarettes "filter" the smoke because of their extra length. If you smoke your cigarette all the way down to the normal inch, or inch-and-a-quarter butt, you are getting more nicotine from that king-size cigarette than you would from a regular one. The cigarette has more tobacco and consequently more nicotine. The king-size has added extra risk instead of protection.

If you smoke only about half of the extra-long cigarette and then put it out, that doesn't help you either. Smoking it halfway down gives you two-thirds as much nicotine and tobacco tar as you find in a regular cigarette. Enough nicotine and tobacco tar are there—enough, in this case, being too much for your health.

MENTHOLATED CIGARETTES ARE NOT 'COOL'

"Cool" mentholated cigarettes contain just as much nicotine and tobacco tars as the regular brands. In addition, these cigarettes contain another irritant—menthol. Menthol produces a sensation of coolness, but it does not lower the temperature of the smoke taken into your mouth. Smoke from a mentholated cigarette will reach a temperature of 190 degrees Fahrenheit, just like any other cigarette.

Because menthol has a stronger taste than tobacco, it kills your awareness of the raw, irritating character of the smoke, but it doesn't change the character of the smoke which remains as raw and irritating as ever.

DENICOTINIZED CIGARETTES ARE A DANGEROUS FAKE

Denicotinized cigarettes *do* contain nicotine, despite the name. They also contain all the tobacco tars.

As you have seen in this and other chapters, the nicotine in a cigarette harms you, regardless of the amount. Never do denicotinized cigarettes contain less than half the nicotine content of regular cigarettes. In many cases, they have almost as much as the standard brands, according to the Journal of the American Medical Association.

No tobacco manufacturer makes a cigarette from which the nicotine has been completely removed. The only place where completely denicotinized cigarettes have been produced are the medical laboratories doing research on smoking. Very few people have ever smoked a cigarette containing absolutely no nicotine. You wouldn't like it if you did.

Since nicotine is what causes addiction to tobacco, it's not surprising that people do not enjoy smoking denicotinized cigarettes. People smoking these cigarettes report that they are extremely harsh and distasteful. The craving for tobacco cannot be satisfied when the nicotine, which causes the craving, is removed.

The reason smokers are able to accept commercial "denicotinized" cigarettes is that they *are* getting the nicotine to which their systems have become addicted. The Federal Trade Commission says it is impossible to remove all the nicotine from tobacco without making it unfit for smoking. Denicotinized cigarettes are especially dangerous because people smoking them kid themselves into thinking they have protection against the dangers of smoking.

'MILDNESS' MEANS NOTHING

Many tobacco manufacturers make claims of "mildness." As used in the ads, the word "mildness" has no meaning. For example, the dark, "strong," Cuban cigarettes contain less nicotine than some of the "mild," denicotinized brands. A leading brand based an advertising campaign on the slogan that it was "milder." Tests proved that it led all other cigarettes in the amount of nicotine.

Thus, we see the so-called protection offered by some brands is no protection at all. Whether you smoke regular cigarettes or the special cigarettes discussed here, you are exposed to all the dangers of smoking.

Filtered cigarettes do as much damage to your system as regular cigarettes. King-size cigarettes are likely to do even more damage; certainly not less. Mentholated cigarettes have an added irritant and are just as hot as the ordinary ones. Denicotinized brands are a dangerous fake. There is only one sure way of protecting yourself against tobacco's nasty effects —stop smoking.

10. Singing Commercial or Funeral Dirge?

A man from Mars, observing all the cigarette advertising, would come to the conclusion that smoking is one of the pleasantest things in the world, also one of the most obnoxious. Each ad boasts of special benefits from smoking a particular brand and implies all others are harsh, irritating, and harmful. As the saying goes, you can't have your cake and eat it too. All cigarettes are made the same way, from the same kinds of tobacco, Either they are pleasant and soothing, or they are harsh, irritating, and harmful.

Having read thus far, you know what the best medical minds in this country say about smoking. The tobacco companies speak otherwise. Supplying tobacco to the public is not a health service but a four billion dollar industry. They are in business to make money. They spend about 61 million dollars a year advertising. You will see in this chapter what they do to sell their products.

GOOD ATHLETES DO NOT SMOKE

It is common knowledge that athletes do not smoke, especially in training. One of the all-time great coaches, Knute Rockne, was dead set against smoking because it slows a player's reflexes. Gene Tunney, Ty Cobb, and many other notables in the sports world, refused to touch tobacco.

You will nevertheless find some who sign testimonials saying they smoke such-and-such a brand. Naturally, they get paid for the use of their names. It's an easy way of earning a fast buck. Cigarettes will never hurt them, they figure, as long as they don't smoke.

A cigarette company was called before the Federal Trade Commission for claiming that smoking gives you a lift. The company produced testimonials. Here are athletes, it said, who praise our brand. It did not claim the athletes smoked the cigarettes, merely that they had signed the testimonials. The company then produced other witnesses, not athletes or medical men, who said that smoking this brand gave them a lift.

The Commission next listened to medical testimony. The doctors maintained it was impossible for smoking to help an athlete, since smoking reduces energy and endurance. After weighing the evidence on both sides, the Commission ordered the claim discontinued as without basis in fact.

ADVERTISERS FALSIFY MEDICAL FACTS

You are bombarded with so much advertising propaganda that you do not examine it as closely as you should. It's time to take a good, long second look. Cigarette ads do not give you straight facts; if they did, they wouldn't sell. Tobacco products are sold by implication and inference, distortion and lies.

One advertisement that you probably recall featured a wise-looking doctor in a white coat (a professional model). The copy stated that after a 30-day period the doctors did not find one case of nose or throat irritation due to smoking "Baileys." While the ad did not promise that smoking "Baileys" would not irritate *your* nose and throat, it left you with the feeling that the company had made some pretty scientific tests.

When challenged by the Federal Trade Commission, the company said, in a letter, it had never claimed that smoking "Baileys" would not harm the throat. It admitted that the doctors had found instances of throat irritation but tried to weasel out by a further involved statement.

In another case before the Commission, supposed experts, who signed cigarette testimonials for a different company, confessed to some astonishing facts. One man, pictured in the ads as a big tobacco grower and plantation owner, proved a poor dirt farmer. He raised a little tobacco on a small plot of ground. Another said he didn't know what he was signing; he couldn't read or write more than his name. He was paid for the testimonial, however, and happy to sign on the dotted line.

Very rarely in the history of the Commission has there been a time when complaints for false advertising were not pending against *all* the major tobacco companies. The worst that can happen is a slap-on-the-wrist order from the Commission telling the company to stop using a particular slogan or claim. As a rule, these cases take about 2 years to be settled. Since they are so drawn out, lawyers can usually protest with wide-eyed innocence that the company has long since stopped using the offending slogan. And so it goes.

ADVERTISING SLOGANS DISTORT THE TRUTH

Let's examine a few of the current slogans. These days, cigarette advertisers try to pound away at the health angle because people are finally beginning to realize what smoking can do to them.

One slogan is featured with testimonials of celebrities and stars (who, naturally, are paid for making these statements). They are pictured as saying they smoke a certain brand of filter tip cigarettes for it is "Just what the doctor ordered."

The implication is that a doctor told them to smoke this brand. We know of no doctor who will advise anyone to smoke, or to switch from one brand to another. We know there is no appreciable difference between brands. And further, we know that filter tips actually give no protection. How, then, can a brand of filter tip cigarettes be "Just what the doctor ordered"?

Consider the slogan of a well-known mentholated cigarette. The opening words of the TV commercial lead you to think the product will help you break the smoking habit. You are told not to be chained to the "hot" cigarette habit. You are advised to switch from a "hot" cigarette to a "cool" one. As you have seen, the temperature of the "cool" mentholated cigarettes is the same as the temperature of the regular cigarettes.

How stupid are you supposed to be? First you get the implication that smoking is an undesirable habit; then you are told to go on smoking. The company doesn't want you to break the cigarette habit; it just wants you to be chained to a "cool" cigarette (which adds menthol to the usual irritants of ordinary brands).

Another major cigarette company has come up with the statement that its product is low in nicotine and high in quality. This is a beautiful example of vague advertising claims which mean exactly nothing. How much nicotine is in this "low" nicotine cigarette? No major brand, including this one, has less than 18 milligrams per cigarette, and *any* nicotine at all is too much. As for the high quality claim, what has quality to do with nicotine, tobacco tars, your health, or anything indeed but selling cigarettes?

There is no slogan advertising tobacco which can bear close examination. Analyze any one of them and you will find empty claims, distortions, and mis-statements.

THE CONSPIRACY OF SILENCE

In spite of the noisy commercials and the long, loud talk about the virtues of this or that cigarette, there is an unusual silence on the harm done by smoking. The newspapers, magazines, radio, and TV are full of news about polio, muscular distrophy, etc. In many cases you are told how to protect yourself or what to do when illness strikes. But when were you warned about exposing yourself to many diseases (besides cancer) by smoking?

Articles show you how to live longer by keeping your weight down. When were you shown that you could live longer by not smoking? Did you ever see an article or listen to a program which said you have a 600% better chance of avoiding a heart attack if you don't smoke?

On rare occasions, unfavorable publicity about smoking does break through. Even then, the subject is handled so gingerly, surrounded by so many *if's, and's,* and *but's* that you don't know what to believe. The recent publicity given to the connection between smoking and cancer is a case in point. Tobacco tars cause cancer, as you have seen. When the news first broke, the initial reports were fairly straightforward.

In the days and weeks that followed, however, there was a rash of articles in newspapers and magazines. These seemed to be written with the purpose of raising questions about the earlier stories. No doubt the public relations agencies for the tobacco companies were at work. The testimony of cancer experts was opposed by statements of doctors who had done little or no research in the field. (Doctors are human beings. You will always be able to find a few to give opinions on a subject about which they know little or nothing.)

THE CONFUSED PUBLIC

Poor John Q. Public reads the conflicting statements and becomes bewildered. He finishes by believing whatever makes him feel most comfortable. It is the easiest way out.

You may ask, why do the publishing and broadcasting industries shy away from publicity unfavorable to the tobacco industry. Better ask why not, when they make almost 61 million dollars a year on tobacco advertising. They don't want to kill the goose that lays those golden advertising eggs. Therefore the conspiracy of silence on the dangers of smoking.

You are now better informed than most smokers. You have all the medical information about smoking at your fingertips. For you, the conspiracy of silence has been broken. The cigarette singing commercial need not become your funeral dirge.

Your Personal Experience with Smoking

1. Remember How You Started

In order to stop smoking, you must recall how you started. Think back to the first cigarette you ever smoked—something like a quarter of a million cigarettes ago. Maybe you had a reason for lighting that first cigarette. Whatever it was, I'll bet you didn't do it for pleasure.

People begin smoking for reasons which have little to do with the so-called pleasures of smoking. When you're in your teens, cigarettes seem to mean maturity. They are a smoke screen to cover awkwardness. They are smoke signals to the rest of the teen-age tribe that the smoker "belongs." Why did *you* start?

THE FIRST CIGARETTE

I remember my first cigarette very well. I started smoking more years ago than I like to admit—at the ripe, old age of 14. A couple of my pals were smoking already, walking around importantly, puffing on cigarettes when the grown-ups could not see them. In their pockets they carried spicy, little cinnamon candies to kill the smell of tobacco on their breath. After spending hours together, the two of them smoking furiously, they'd pop candies into their mouths just before they left.

Some weeks of teasing by the other two was all I could take. I'll show them, I cried, indignantly and fearfully one night. The next day I demanded a cigarette when Beansie lit one up. He offered me a squashed, wrinkled specimen from his pocket. I took it boldly and struck a match. I pulled the smoke into my mouth with a quick, nervous puff and blew it out again just as quickly. It stung my tongue, my nose smarted, my eyes started to tear from the acrid smoke. Trying to ignore the unpleasantness, I pulled on the cigarette again, drawing the smoke into my lungs.

That did it—I almost doubled over. My windpipe and chest felt as though they had been scraped on a grater. Harsh and rasping smoke was touching the tender, delicate tissues of my lungs for the first time. Pride made me try to keep my distress from my two pals, but it was impossible. I coughed retchingly. I couldn't breathe and my stomach was churning.

Beansie hit me on the back. "Don't let it getcha, boy. It always happens the first time." With Beansie's encouragement, I managed to smoke about two-thirds of the cigarette before I dashed out and was violently sick at my stomach.

Beansie was right. The reaction to tobacco is always full of discomfort or worse, the first time. Your first experience with smoking was probably different, but you didn't enjoy it, did you?

There is a physical reason why the body reacts so violently. Your tissues have never been exposed to the poisonous nicotine before that first cigarette. (If the liver didn't take a part of the nicotine out of general circulation immediately, the first cigarette could even kill you.) Although the liver springs into action right away, it certainly doesn't remove enough nicotine to keep the rest of your body happy. Your tissues are used to plenty of oxygen and nourishment. Suddenly deprived, they act up, sending distress signals.

Dizziness comes from the lessened blood supply to the brain. Irritated and hurt by the smoke, your lungs convulse into coughs to expel the offending smoke. Your stomach rebels against the nasty effect of the nicotine and tries to heave it out, creating waves of nausea, and even making you throw up.

Your body stops acting this way after a few more assaults of tobacco. Not that your system gets used to it! You never develop a tolerance for tobacco. You never develop an immunity to nicotine and the rest of the smoke. Your body ceases to send warning signals; it has become habituated to smoking, but the smoke goes right on harming you.

I started smoking because I had to do what the other guys did. I hated it in the beginning, but I wouldn't admit it. Not to smoke meant being exposed to scorn and ridicule, or so I thought.

CIGARETTES MEAN MATURITY—WHEN YOU'RE 15

Almost always people begin smoking for reasons which have little to do with pleasure. What was your reason? How did you start? In the minds of many young people, cigarettes are a symbol of maturity. As a youngster, you use every device to make yourself seem more mature. To prove that you should be treated like an adult, you consciously adopt an adult habit —smoking. You don't want the cigarette; you want to prove you are grown-up. In most cases smoking starts at a pretty early age, when it is so hard and so important to prove your maturity. In my time it was only the boys who began smoking around 14 and 15; nowadays both boys and girls smoke in their early teens.

AN ACT OF DESPERATION AGAINST AWKWARDNESS

Awkwardness is the opposite of maturity. It is the awkwardness of your middle teens which makes you clutch desperately at cigarettes. Your feet are too big, your arms too long! What to do with them, where to put them? On dates, the start of an evening can be torture. What do you say? What do you do? You seize on smoking as an escape. The ritual of taking out a cigarette, lighting it, and holding it in your hand gives you something to do. Is this smoking for enjoyment? It is blowing a smoke screen to hide confusion. The first cigarette is unpleasant, but you continue out of desperation.

CIGARETTES ARE A BID TO BELONG

At this age, there's something else as important as being grown-up; it is the need to belong to the group and do what the group does. If most of your friends smoke, you feel you must too. You start smoking because you don't want to feel like an outsider, not because you like cigarettes.

Maybe you took the first puff on a dare. Maybe you didn't want to smoke, but even more strongly you didn't want to be called a sissy. That's smoking out of fear.

Most of the kids in my group—like today's teen-agers— imagined smoking made us into adults. I was thinking about that when I decided to give up smoking. Do I still have to go on proving to the world that I'm a mature, independent guy by smoking? At the age of 44, does burning 40 cigarettes a day make me socially acceptable? The thought brought forth a sheepish grin and an admission that these were pretty poor reasons for smoking now.

YOU HAVE A BEAR BY THE TAIL

There is an old story about a tenderfoot who trapped a bear. In order to prove his right to belong to the group of experienced hunters, and in order to display his daring, he grabbed the bear by the tail. Then he started thinking about what would happen when he let go.

The bear was growling, snarling, and lunging ferociously. The tenderfoot grew more and more frightened. If he released the bear, it would attack him; but he couldn't go on holding the bear's tail forever.

It's the same story with smoking. Once you've started, you're afraid to stop. Your present reasons for smoking are probably completely different from the reasons you had for lighting that first cigarette.

The teen-ager grabs the bear's tail. He must prove sophistication and daring to his contemporaries by smoking. When he reaches his late twenties and thirties, he doesn't have to do this any more. He has discovered it wasn't smoking which made his seniors seem older and wiser. It was just that they had lived longer and learned more in the process of living.

By the time he is an adult, however, smoking is a fixed habit and he's afraid he can't give it up. Now he doesn't dare stop smoking. He doesn't know what will happen if he tries. He has a bear by the tail and he can't let go.

But you don't have to sigh hopelessly and reach for a cigarette. This is where your story ceases to be like the sad case of the tenderfoot and the bear. This story—my story, your story—has a happy ending. In the following chapters you will learn exactly what to do. You can stop smoking by following a simple procedure. You'll see how to adapt this procedure to your own needs and personality.

You have already begun by recalling your reactions to your first cigarette. You are wise enough now to discount the drives that made you start smoking. Cigarettes can't make you seem any more mature—you are mature. You know that desperate puffing at a cigarette *reveals* rather than *conceals* awkwardness. You are aware that a habitual smoker has a bear by the tail. The following chapters will show you how to let him go.

2. Why You Smoke

Once you know why you started smoking, your next stop is to find out why you smoke now. Occasionally you say to yourself, "I ought to cut down. My wind isn't what it used to be." The morning after a big party you think about it. You smoked a lot and maybe drank more than you meant to. Your head aches. Your throat feels raw. There's a nasty taste in your mouth. You light up a cigarette, take a puff, and put it out angrily because it makes you feel even worse. When you think about smoking ordinarily, these things don't occur to you. You consider smoking one of the pleasures of life.

While I was still smoking, one of my friends, a non-smoker, asked me, "Why do you smoke, anyway?"

"Because I like to," said I, shrugging my shoulders.

Afterwards I started thinking about it and I came up with some surprising facts. What I thought were my reasons for smoking weren't the real reasons at all. I *didn't start* smoking for pleasure! It was an unpleasant experience. How did smoking turn into a pleasurable experience over the years? Or did it—really?

Take the average smoker who thinks he is smoking for pleasure (not the one who recognizes he is in the grip of a habit). Ask him why he smokes and he'll give you reasons like the following:

> Smoking helps you relax.
> You blow your troubles away in smoke.
> Smoking passes the time.
> Smoking is fun.
> It helps you think.
> Smoking is a reward and it rounds out many pleasures.

A cigarette is a companion when you're alone.
It gives you something to do with your hands.
It gives you a lift.

Now let's examine these reasons and see what's behind them.

SMOKING DOES NOT HELP YOU RELAX

Before you go in to ask the boss for a raise, you want to
smoke. While your wife's having a baby, you pace the floor,
inhaling puff after puff. You're waiting to hear what the doctor says about that pain in your heart, and you light up your
pipe. You are standing before the judge hoping it won't be a
$25.00 fine for speeding, and you finger the cigarettes in your
pocket and wish you were allowed to smoke in court.

Whenever you find yourself in a situation that makes you
feel strained and nervous, you smoke if you possibly can.
After you finish the first cigarette, you still feel nervous and
tense because the situation hasn't changed. You light another
cigarette and you finish that one too, and a third, and a fourth!
You are becoming jumpier than a cat. As a matter of fact,
you're more nervous than you were when you lit your first cigarette.

Smoking hasn't relaxed you. Remember the chapter on
smoking and day-to-day living! Remember what nicotine does
to the nerves and the brain, which is the nerve center! There's
less blood going to your brain, and you're developing a headache. Your nerves are taut as stretched rubber-bands, ready to
snap any minute, and smoking increases your tension.

Suppose the circumstances dissolve the tension. The nurse
comes out, taps you on the shoulder, and says, "Mother and
child are fine. You have a wonderful, healthy, new son." What
do you do? You dash the cigarette down on the floor. What
you needed was the good news to make you relax; all the
cigarettes in the world couldn't do it.

Or, perhaps, after the doctor finishes his check-up, he beck-
ons you from the waiting room where you were pulling anx-
iously at a hot pipe. When you walk into his office, he smiles
at you. "There's nothing to worry about," he says. "That pain
comes from overeating—not the heart. Your heart's in good

shape for a man of your age." You feel the tension flow from your body. Unconsciously, you knock out the pipe in the ashtray. It doesn't taste very good, and what do you need it for anyway? You're relaxed at last, but it wasn't the pipe that helped you; it was the doctor's good news.

In a dramatic way, these incidents give the lie to one of the common myths about tobacco. You think of it as an aid to relaxation in tense situations. The exact opposite is true—smoking increases tension. The athlete who wants steady nerves and accurate judgment doesn't light up a cigarette just before he runs out on the field.

YOU DON'T HAVE TO SMOKE TO FORGET YOUR TROUBLES

"I can sit in my chair and blow my troubles away in the smoke," you say. "I inhale deeply. As I blow out the smoke I watch it swirl and eddy about the room. I stare at the smoke curling from my cigarette in the ashtray; it circles the lamp base before it spirals up through the shade. I watch it and forget all my troubles for 10 minutes."

What you say is true and untrue at the same time. Yes, you forget all your troubles for 10 minutes; but it isn't the smoking that does it. You forget your troubles because you are concentrating on something else. You can use the same system to forget your troubles without smoking. You don't need a cigarette to work it.

The essence of your system is concentration. Instead of smoking a cigarette and concentrating on it, focus all your attention on anything else that interests you for 10 or 15 minutes. Choose something that doesn't call for any effort on your part. If you like children, stand at the window and watch kids playing in the street.

After I stopped smoking, I used to sit in my favorite chair and stare at a big mirror hanging on the wall. It was opposite a smaller mirror on the other wall and reflected the image of the smaller mirror many times. I would try to count the number of times the smaller mirror was repeated in the reflection I was looking at. Once I got as far as 11—before I happened to look at my watch. I had been concentrating on the damn thing for almost 20 minutes. All my troubles had vanished in the reflections of that mirror.

Obviously, it isn't exhaling the smoke that blows your troubles away. Concentrating on any object outside yourself does the trick. A cigarette is definitely not required.

SMOKING MAKES TIME MOVE SLOWLY

There is another reason people give for smoking—it passes the time. Waiting for someone, standing in line to get into a show, sitting restlessly in the stands before the first race starts or the first ball is pitched, pacing up and down the station waiting for the train that's late—waiting, waiting, waiting— what do you do when you're waiting? Most smokers light up a cigarette or a pipe or a cigar; it helps to pass the time.

Take a careful look at that last statement; it's a clever piece of self-deception. Smoking makes you more conscious of how slowly time moves. If you hate waiting, let's see whether smoking makes waiting easier. You are already nervous because you have to wait. Smoking will make you more nervous. As you become more nervous, the time will move even more slowly. Perhaps waiting makes you angry. Anger stimulates the adrenal glands, just as nicotine does. You want to quiet those upset adrenals and calm your anger to make the waiting more bearable; smoking stirs them even more.

The easy-going person doesn't fare any better when he smokes to pass the time. He says, "Waiting is boring. If I smoke, I'll have something to do." He uses the sigarette to make bargains with the time. "When I finish this cigarette," he promises himself, "the bus will come," or "the game will start," or, "my friend will get here."

I don't have to point out that the cigarette isn't a magic war 1. You can wave your cigarette at the clock all you want. The game isn't going to start until the umpire yells, "Play ball!" If your friend is 20 minutes away, smoking that cigarette won't make him arrive in 10 minutes. Because you're smoking to pass the time, smoking makes you concentrate on time and how slowly it's moving. Find something else in your immediate surroundings that you can watch or think about, and you will see how much faster time passes.

CHILDREN LIKE TO PLAY WITH FIRE—DO YOU?

Is smoking a game to you? Is it fun? I asked myself these questions when I thought about giving up smoking. The answer I came up with was, "Yes!" I wouldn't admit it to anybody else, but I did have the honesty to admit it to myself. Here was I, a grown man, with a wife and two children, still playing with matches and cigarette lighters.

Everybody is fascinated by fire. When I smoked, there was something satisfying in flicking the little wheel of my lighter and seeing the flame respond to my touch. I used to bawl out my son for playing with my lighter. "You're using up the flint, making the fluid evaporate!" Even though I didn't let him know it, I understood why he got a kick out of working the lighter, because I did too.

Like most Americans, I'm fond of gadgets. I boasted about my lighter. "It always works," I would say. I could be reading in a comfortable chair with my lighter on the table beside me. Glancing at it made me reach for my cigarettes. I didn't really want one but I wanted to use the lighter. Like my son, I liked to play with it. Out came the cigarette, flick went the wheel, and the flame sprang into life. It was fun.

True, I didn't enjoy the cigarette, but it was part of a comforting game I was still playing unconsciously. As a youngster, smoking was a piece of play-acting magic. In my early years, smoking turned me into an adult—or so I thought. True, I didn't enjoy the taste of the cigarette or the effects of the smoke. But I wasn't smoking because I liked it; becoming more grown-up (in my own mind) was what I liked. At 44, I was still unconsciously thinking of the pleasure I achieved from my youthful pretense. It wasn't the cigarette I was enjoying; it was the memory of what the cigarette had meant when I was a kid; and here I was, still seeking to recapture it at age 44. I felt pretty silly when I thought it all out.

SMOKING INTERFERES WITH THINKING

Many people dread giving up smoking because they feel they will lose an aid to thinking. Does smoking help you think? It gives you headaches on occasion, it causes memory lapses, it tires you faster and makes you more nervous—great help when you're trying to think!

You've got a little game going with the boys in your outfit! Is that So-and-So bluffing, or does he have an inside straight? You're sitting at your desk figuring out your income tax. Why do the figures get all balled up? In either case you're stuck. Your hand reaches for a smoke even though there's an unpleasant taste in your mouth. The cigarette is hot and dry, and your throat is raw. As you light your cigarette, you stop thinking about your problem for a moment. Giving your brain a momentary break is very helpful because you have been trying too hard. Suddenly you see what you missed; the mistake in addition hits you in the eye. You've got those income tax blues licked. Or the little puzzle at the poker table straightens out; the breather gave you a chance to realize he was bluffing. The cigarette didn't make the situation clear; the momentary relaxation did.

You have conditioned yourself to associate smoking with thinking, although they don't have any real connection. Sit back and name the various places where you think without a cigarette. Perhaps you work in an office or a shop where smoking is forbidden. Would you say, therefore, you can't think while you're working? If you didn't think while you worked, you wouldn't hold your job very long.

When I first swore off smoking, I needed a substitute for my writing hours. I hit on the scheme of keeping a crossword puzzle in my desk. If my brain suddenly ran dry, I took out the puzzle and worked at it 10 or 15 minutes. It did the trick. I had a breather and I could turn back to my typewriter and find the word that didn't come 10 minutes ago. It's the short period of relaxation which is important—not the cigarette.

YOU DON'T HAVE TO REWARD YOURSELF 30 TIMES A DAY

The need for relaxation also gives rise to the "reward" system of smoking. The woman doing the breakfast dishes promises herself a cigarette the moment the dishes are put away. The salesman bringing out the seventh pair of shoes wonders how much longer it will take to satisfy his customer. "What a beaut she is! Seven more pairs to go—I know it!" says Joe. "I sure will deserve that cigarette if I ever get it." Reward smokers use the cigarette as a present to themselves for finishing an unpleasant job. It's relaxation. It breaks the day into 20 or 30 occasions when you reward yourself with a cigarette. As a child, you got rewards for being good, but certainly not as many as that! Anyway, are you still a child? Do you really have to pat ourself on the back 20 or 30 times a day?

SMOKING DOESN'T ROUND OUT OTHER PLEASURES

Many smokers will protest that they smoke to "round out" other pleasures. The perfect end to a good meal, they say, is a good cigarette or a fine cigar. Listening to the radio or watching your favorite TV program, it's nice to sit back, puffing on a pipe.

If you smoke for enjoyment, you can make yourself comfortable in an attempt to "enjoy" that smoke. When you go to a movie, you watch it from the stuffy, smoking section, if the theatre has one. Otherwise you sneak out between features for a cigarette. It's a shame to miss the cartoon, but you must have a cigarette to round out the movie.

The cigarette after a meal rounds out the pleasure of eating, or so you think. Doesn't it subdue that full, stuffed feeling and take away the heavy food taste? Perhaps you're using the cigarette to conceal from yourself the fact that you eat too much! Cigarettes take away the taste of food. They also destroy much of your sense of smell which contributes to your enjoyment of good flavors. How then do they round out the pleasures of a good meal?

When you're watching a TV program and enjoying it, doesn't the cigarette smoulder in the ashtray? If you grow bored, you begin smoking again. The next time you smoke, ask yourself how much you are enjoying the cigarette. What about the after-taste the cigarette leaves in your mouth? What about the smoker's cough? And the rawness of your throat? Smoking doesn't really increase your enjoyment of other pleasures.

YOU ARE BETTER COMPANY FOR YOURSELF THAN A CIGARETTE

Perhaps smoking provides you with company when you are alone. You light up a cigarette, sit back, and watch the smoke. The blue haze makes a friendly barrier against the emptiness of the room. The cigarette or pipe is the silent friend who keeps you company.

Having read the first section, you know what dangerous company you are keeping. This friendly tobacco and the lazy, spiraling smoke are invading your body. The "innocent" cigarette carries discomfort, illness, disaster, and even death. Is this a friend to welcome?

When I gave up smoking, I adopted another companion to keep me company when I was alone. I became a friend to myself. No more sitting down and staring at a little tube of white paper stuffed with tobacco! Now I had 15 minutes to spend with myself. Like everybody else I have a lot of faults, but this 15-minute period was not the time to think about them.

If you are with a friend, you don't sit and think about his faults. You enjoy the things which make him a likeable person. I was keeping myself company. This was the time to remember something of which I was proud. I contemplated some of my good qualities. I thought about my virtues—not my weaknesses. Try it sometime when you're alone. It's a pleasant experience—worth repeating every so often. It refreshes you and takes the edge off a lot of problems.

YOU DON'T NEED A CIGARETTE AS A CRUTCH

Sometimes you lean on a crutch which is about 2¾ of an inch long—that's the length of a regular cigarette. Not very substantial! At social gatherings many people feel the need of something to do with their hands. Holding a cigarette allays nervousness. Puffing on a pipe offers a little time to think of something to say. Offering a cigarette breaks the ice and provides an opening for conversation. These are common explanations.

Now I've found the "awkward" pause, the "awkward" silence, really aren't so awkward after all. You do talk to people at parties; you don't keep offering your new acquaintance a cigarette every 5 minutes to keep up the conversation. Whatever you talk about, you'll continue discussing after smoking the cigarette, or you'll say without the cigarette. The cigarette doesn't start the conversation—you do. You have been carrying on conversations all your life—not the cigarettes you smoked.

SMOKING DOESN'T GIVE YOU A LIFT

What about the "lift" smokers swear by? Is that the reason you give for smoking? (The doctors say it's impossible for smoking to give you a lift.) You're tired; you've been working hard all day. (The doctors say smoking cuts down your energy and endurance—remember?) As soon as you get into the house, you sink down into your comfortable chair and light up a cigarette. As the first deep drag hits your solar plexus, you feel better. But it's not a lift—it's relief, isn't it?

Analyze the sensation carefully. Doesn't that first puff soothe a kind of gnawing feeling down in your chest cavity? After the first couple of drags, this peculiar hunger has been satisfied but you automatically finish the cigarette. The first two or three puffs give you the lift that people talk about; but it really is the satisfaction of the body's hunger for a drug. Nicotine is the drug and you are a drug addict.

Wait a minute—don't fly off the handle! I just want to explain the source of the lift. I'm not saying this is a horrible and pitiful condition, like morphine or heroin addiction. It doesn't make you a menace to society or wreck the lives of everyone around you. If smoking breaks down your health or shortens your life, well—it's your life.

There's a big difference between addiction to nicotine and addiction to other drugs. In one respect, breaking the craving for nicotine is a cinch compared to the effort it takes to break the morphine habit, for example. You don't experience anything like the terrible condition of denarcotization which the morphine addict goes through when deprived of his drug. Your "hunger" for the next cigarette (created by the last one you smoked) consists of a vague restlessness—nothing more serious than that.

Once you've stopped smoking, your body's addiction to nicotine stops in a very short time. It takes only a few days—a week at the most. If you take a cigarette after you have definitely stopped smoking, your body will react as it did to your first cigarette. The cigarette will taste like straw and burnt rags. You'll probably get dizzy and feel nauseous. Your body loses the craving and tolerance for nicotine very rapidly. If you stop smoking, you no longer want to smoke.

SMOKING DRAGS YOU DOWN

The reasons given for smoking don't hold up very well when they are examined in broad daylight. Smoking doesn't help you relax. It increases tension, nervousness, keeps you from going to sleep, and gives you headaches. Do you blow your troubles away in smoke? No, you forget your troubles for a while because you're concentrating on one object. Solid concentration on something outside yourself—not necessarily a cigarette—for 10 or 15 minutes will do the trick.

Smoking passes the time, you said. Exactly the opposite! Smoking makes you more conscious of how slowly time is passing. Do you smoke because it's fun? You aren't 16 any more; why use a teen-ager's reason for smoking?

Does smoking help you think? Changing the focus of your attention helps you think—not the cigarette. If you have been concentrating on one subject hard and long, don't smoke—take a break. You will come back to your problem refreshed. Are you the person who uses smoking as a reward? Do you really want to pat yourself on the back 20 or 30 times a day?

If you claim a cigarette rounds out other pleasures, think of how many times you make yourself uncomfortable in order to smoke. Or, how many times you smoke because you are uncomfortable, not for pleasure. To keep loneliness away, you smoke when no one is around you. You are much better company for yourself than a piece of paper stuffed with tobacco. Thinking about things you have accomplished provides you with a very pleasant atmosphere. It stops the loneliness and takes the edge off your problems as a cigarette never could.

Smoking drags you down; it doesn't give you a lift. You are only trying to satisfy the body's hunger for a drug by smoking. What shall you do with your hands? Once you stop leaning on the cigarette as a crutch in social situations, you will find that you get along just as well without it. You will realize that you can talk just as well or better without puffing on a cigarette.

There is a primary reason for smoking not yet considered. Everything mentioned in this chapter is linked with it. All the factors in smoking, described in this chapter, are tied up with the fact that smoking is nothing more than a very strong habit. Any habit that *you* have formed, *you* can break!

3. Are You Smoking Against Your Will

If you go through a pack or more a day, smoking is a compulsive habit. I was a two-pack man myself. The majority of smokers are compulsive smokers. Human beings are creatures of habit and smoking lays a strong hold upon you; it compels you to go through certain actions and rituals each day. Even though smokers often give reasons for smoking, like those mentioned in the last chapter, such reasons are usually excuses.

Most people are actually smoking *against their will*. Excuses for smoking are part of the habit pattern, the ritual of smoking. Smoking has become an automatic act.

WHAT IS YOUR PATTERN OF SMOKING?

You are ready to figure out where you stand. Begin by recalling your physical sensations when you smoked your first cigarette. Continue by analysing your present smoking habits. That's all. Just be honest with yourself. To give you an idea of how to go about it, I'll show you what I discovered when I analysed my own smoking habits. You will probably find many similarities in your pattern of smoking.

As soon as I woke up in the morning, even before getting out of bed, I lit up a cigarette. (*With a cumpulsive smoker like me, beginning something—anything, calls for a cigarette.*) I couldn't face the thought of getting up without one. Very often I would smoke two while lying in bed. Then into the bathroom to wash and shave. I looked forward to brushing my teeth because it was the only time in the day when my mouth felt fresh and clean.

As soon as I finished, I had to light up a cigarette. It was so pleasant to smoke with a fresh mouth. Besides, I had just finished doing something. *When you end an activity, you have to smoke.* Returning to the bedroom, I proceeded to dress, with a cigarette burning in the ashtray. Getting dressed was a new activity and I had to have a cigarette to go with it.

Finishing my breakfast, I would light my fifth cigarette to go with my coffee. Cigarettes and coffee go together like . . .

like . . . cigarettes and coffee! If I had time for two cups of coffee, I smoked two cigarettes. As soon as I closed the door behind me, and stepped into the elevator, I drew out a cigarette automatically. I was doing something different by leaving. *Obviously the change of pace demanded the cigarette I lit without thinking.*

After I settled myself under the wheel, and as I was waiting those few seconds for the motor to warm up, I naturally lit a cigarette. I was waiting, wasn't I? Driving in the annoying stop-and-go rhythm of city traffic or waiting for a red light to change was the signal for another cigarette.

Arrival in the office called for a cigarette. I smoked the next one, sitting at my desk going over the mail. It was a new activity in the day. By 10 o'clock in the morning, I had managed to go through more than half a pack. And so it went for the rest of the day. It was a ritual I followed unthinkingly for more than 20 years.

SMOKING IS AUTOMATIC

Smoking is a habit associated with many stimuli. Some stimuli are the same for all people; others vary from person to person. In the preceding paragraphs, I mentioned some of the stimuli which made me reach for a cigarette.

These stimuli may generally be classified as changes in tempo, the performance of specific activities, the body's "hunger" for nicotine (because of addiction to the drug), and the sight of others smoking.

A change in tempo may mean going from one task to another in the house, going inside from out-of-doors, etc. Performing a specific activity like drinking coffee, or reading the paper, can be the stimulus which makes you want to smoke. The body's hunger for nicotine—although it cannot be described exactly—is easy to recognize, and needs no definition for the smoker. The stimulus of sight is one with which we are all familiar. You see somebody smoking and you light up a cigarette. Smoking in this fashion is compulsive, not pleasure smoking.

Examine yourself honestly if you think you are one of those smokers who have a "reason" for smoking. Aren't you smoking in the same way, at the same times, for the same reasons, each day? Don't specific activities call for a cigarette? Your body responds to a certain stimulus—you pull out the pack and light up. What are you doing? You are following a compulsive habit pattern.

The compulsive smoker goes through his one or two packs a day without the excuses that lighter smokers sometimes give, the excuses of the previous chapter. Smoking one cigarette after another, you wish they didn't taste so bad. Occasionally you put one out before you've finished it. Half an hour later, that vague, annoying sensation begins. It won't be quieted unless you light another cigarette. You don't want it, but you smoke it anyway.

At a party, you're talking to a friend and he pulls out a cigarette. Either he offers you one, and you take it automatically, or you smoke one of your own automatically. You didn't want the cigarette, but the sight of someone else smoking made you follow suit. Let's face it! You are living under a dictatorship. You have your own personal tyrant—the cigarette. This is automatic smoking.

What is your exact habit pattern? Before you go any further, establish it clearly in your mind. Think of all the occasions which lead *you* to light a cigarette. Ask yourself when was the last time you really enjoyed a cigarette—if you ever did?

YOU SMOKE WHEN YOU DON'T WANT TO

You are living under such tyranny that you smoke even though you experience unpleasant physical symptoms from doing so. The food you eat doesn't have much flavor. You have a perpetual bad taste in your mouth. Your tongue feels furry and fuzzy. Your sense of smell (part of food's good taste comes from its appetizing odors) is cut down. Your vision isn't as good as it might be. You are nervous and it takes you a long time to fall asleep.

Smokers are so accustomed to living with these symptoms, they begin to believe that nervousness, sleeplessness, a bad appetite, and unpleasant taste in the mouth are a part of their physical make-up.

When you feel miserable—your head aches, your nose is stopped up, your throat is raw, or you have a bad cold—you don't want to smoke; still you light up a cigarette. It tastes 10 times worse than it usually does; nonetheless, you go ahead and smoke. The cigarette tastes so bad and it bothers you so much, you put it out and promise yourself you are not going to smoke another. Half an hour later, you light up a cigarette, swearing at your own weakness. Even though you don't want to, you are smoking.

CIGARETTES RULE YOU

Consider some of the other aspects of this dictatorship under which you live. Cigarettes force you to undergo all kinds of unpleasantness. Is your job one where you can't smoke while working? Then you spend many of your working hours thinking, "In 2 hours . . . in 1 hour . . . in 10 minutes, I can smoke." You suffer in a place where smoking is not allowed. Instead of concentrating on what you want to do, you keep thinking about smoking.

If you're caught without cigarettes, you feel extremely uncomfortable, even desperate. In the dead of winter, on the coldest night, you put on your coat and go outside to buy a pack. Maybe you get in your car and drive miles for the cigarettes. What for? They will only keep you from falling asleep —later in the evening. If—Heaven forbid!—you can't get any cigarettes, you go around like a down-and-outer, picking stale, old butts from the ashtrays, lighting them, burning your lips, choking on the foul taste, but smoking.

When the hunger for nicotine, when this addiction says "Jump!" you jump. You are afraid to be without cigarettes. You're not your own boss any longer. You haven't control of the situation; the cigarettes have.

SMOKING IS HARD ON YOUR BUDGET

There is another obvious disadvantage to smoking; it costs money—more and more every year. Gone are the days when you paid 10 or 12 cents a pack. With the money we have saved by not smoking, my wife and I have managed to see the whole World Series. We've gone to more shows and treated ourselves to little luxuries we couldn't afford before.

I used to smoke 2 packs a day, and my wife, 1 pack. Together we spent 300 dollars a year on cigarettes. If you smoke a pack a day, you spend almost 100 dollars a year. That doesn't take into account the money you spend on lighters, cigarette cases, and all the accessories to smoking.

This figure doesn't include the tailor's bills either. How many holes have cigarettes made in your suits? A live coal drops down and burns itself out unnoticed. Anywhere between 5 and 10 dollars for a re-weaving job. More frequent cleanings are necessary because ashes scatter over your clothes. You can never brush away the smudge ashes leave on dark suits and dresses. And did you add to the cost of smoking all the damage done to furniture by cigarettes—burns on wood, holes in the upholstery? The figure mounts up. Eliminate smoking and you give your budget a welcome increase, without even putting in any overtime.

TOBACCO DESTROYS SEX APPEAL AND GLAMOUR

The expense of smoking is not the worst drawback, by a long shot. Tobacco smoke leaves a heavy odor which clings to your clothes and your breath. While I was still smoking, my wife often shrank from my evening greeting. She'd wrinkle up her nose and say, "Darling, you smell like . . . like a tobacco factory. What'd you do? Roll in it?"

As I bent down to kiss her, she would turn her head away. "I'm sorry, but your breath practically knocks me over," she confessed reluctantly. "I almost hate to have you kiss me after you've been smoking." I couldn't argue with her. Tobacco breath isn't a pleasant atmosphere for a close-up or a clinch. Kissing someone who smells like an ashtray full of old butts doesn't help romance.

The sallow smoker's skin isn't any help either. The woman who is worried about those new, little wrinkles, and the yellow pallor of her skin has a much better chance of improving her appearance if she throws away her cigarettes. Smoking affects your health, and your general state of health affects your skin. Skin changes occur from the inside. All the creams and lotions, applied to the outside, don't change your appearance; they preserve it as it is. Giving up smoking actually changes your skin from within.

Like beauty, poise and sophistication also come from within. Smoking doesn't make you seem more poised. Frenzied fumbling for cigarettes at social functions is not a sign of so-phistication. As a teen-ager, awkward and unsure of yourself, you used to hope that smoking would cover up lack of poise. Ability to blow smoke in someone else's face is no measure of confidence. If you feel ill at ease, it's consoling to remember that the other person probably does too. Frantic smoking will make it obvious to everyone that you are unsure of yourself. Don't smoke, and it's much easier to keep your secret.

QUITTING IS NOT A TEST OF WILL POWER

You may feel a little frightened at this juncture. You are convinced that you'd like to stop smoking, but afraid you'll fail if you try. Whether you know it or not, you're on your way to freeing yourself from the tyranny of smoking. If the thought of smoking bothers you, even once in a while, or if interest has led you to read the book up to this point, you've made a step—a big step—in the right direction.

Stop saying, "I'd like to stop smoking, but I can't." Stop thinking, "I'm afraid I'll fail." Stop reproaching yourself because you feel you're not quite man or woman enough to carry out this resolve. Curiously, it is the tyranny of the smoking habit which has led you to feel you have no will power and has lowered your own opinion of yourself.

You don't need will power to stop smoking. It's not a matter of will power at all. Even if you tried unsuccessfully before, you *can* stop this time for good, providing you don't make it a test of will power. You probably failed in the past because you didn't know the right way to go about it. Now you have a simple, easy procedure to follow.

You have seen that you have a pattern of smoking—smoking is a habit. You smoke automatically. Even though it is unpleasant to you, you have continued to smoke. The cigarettes rule you. The cost of smoking burdens your budget. Smoking cannot give you poise. It destroys sex appeal. It creates fear of failure because giving up the smoking habit is mistakenly posed as a question of will power.

Now you know, however, what smoking does to your body. You are ready to learn how to break the habit. Before you read any further, take your first step. Make a list, on a card, of the 10 most disagreeable aspects of smoking; put down *your* 10 reasons for disliking smoking. Don't be satisfied with listing them in your mind. Write them down; carry the list around with you wherever you go.

At this point, tell yourself you will stop smoking soon. Don't set your deadline yet; just think of it as in the near future.

How To Stop Smoking

1. A New World of Freedom Awaits You

You know what smoking does to your health. You have analyzed your reasons for smoking and found that you are tied to a habit. You have decided that you are going to quit smoking sometime soon. You're headed for an exhilarating experience.

Giving up smoking will open an exciting new world of freedom for you. Reformed smokers, myself included, can tell you what a wonderful change is in store for you. Constantly keep in mind the picture of this new world. The description of the new pleasures and freedoms that await you is truthful. It is based on the experience of many, many ex-smokers. When the going seems difficult, remember what you are striving for! Think of the five freedoms you win as an ex-smoker.

By giving up smoking you preserve your health and lengthen your life. The annoyances caused by tobacco addiction disappear; you are free of the dictatorship of the cigarette. You're able to do more things with less effort. Your senses become keener and sharper, increasing your enjoyment of life. You are more poised and more confident—ready to face future tasks with new-found strength.

FREEDOM FROM ILLNESS

The first freedom eliminates the constant threat of illness which smoking inflicts upon you. You are helping ward off serious diseases like ulcers, cancer, and heart trouble—to name a few. You are giving yourself a present of extra years of life, healthy, productive years. The whole first section of this book describes the dangers that dog your footsteps as long as you smoke.

Giving up smoking not only protects your health, it also

brings immediate rewards that are demonstrated in an improved physical condition. You're not as old as you thought. Try running up a flight of stairs or sprinting for a bus, you don't puff and gasp any more. When you put on an extra spurt of energy, your heart doesn't protest the way it used to.

FREEDOM FROM ANNOYANCE

In this world from which you have banished the tyrannical cigarette, you are free from all the annoyances that used to attend your smoking. That hacking cigarette cough which bothered you from the time you got up to the time you went to bed is a thing of the past.

Colds don't plague you four or five times a winter. You have gotten rid of that post-nasal drip which made the phlegm run down the back of your throat, choking and irritating you. Your sinuses don't ache in cold, damp weather.

Your mouth feels fresher, smoother, cleaner, no more bad taste and furry tongue. Watch the circulation in your hands and feet during the cold weather. The cold won't bother you the way it did when you were smoking. It's all part of your second freedom. It's a new feeling of vitality, energy, and well-being. You gain it almost as soon as you give up smoking.

FREEDOM FROM FATIGUE

For the first time in many years, you will discover how much energy you really have. You'll be able to do more than you ever could while you were smoking. Things you were putting off for tomorrow because you were too tired, will get done today.

You'll go through the days feeling more alive than you have for a long time. This increase in energy will answer the fear some of you may have about putting on weight. Whatever increase in appetite you experience is temporary. Besides, your extra energy will consume the couple of pounds you may put on in the beginning.

In the world of the ex-smoker, the day begins easily. You're free from tobacco-tiredness. You accomplish more and feel less fatigue.

FREEDOM FOR FULL ENJOYMENT, WITH ALL FIVE SENSES

By giving up smoking, you are making yourself a present of many positive pleasures. The ex-smoker gets more joy out of day-to-day living. His five senses are not dulled and blunted by the effects of smoking upon his system.

Sight improves. That makes your job easier and your recreation more fun. Smoking is no longer a threat to your hearing. Impaired circulation can no longer blunt your sense of touch. If your sense of touch is sharpened, that improves your co-ordination.

After you stop smoking, food tastes better than it ever did before. You can really appreciate the flavor of good, simple food; the fascinating gourmet dishes are more appetizing than they ever were. You'll find out, too, that a kiss tastes different and nicer when stale, smelly tobacco doesn't linger on the breath.

The non-smoker and the ex-smoker have a much keener sense of smell. The tang of fresh air, the perfume of a pretty woman, or a mouth-watering aroma from chocolate cake in the oven give you pleasures you had forgotten you could enjoy.

No more hot, raw smoke to stupefy your senses. You have freedom for full enjoyment of living with all your five senses.

FREEDOM FOR FUTURE ACHIEVEMENT

You have gained poise and confidence by throwing off a deeply ingrained habit like smoking. You feel proud of your own strength because you have made yourself the master of your habits. They no longer lead you around by the nose. Conquering a habit like smoking makes you the master. It's an exhilarating, satisfying feeling that is well deserved.

You can now do what you want. You have learned how to manage yourself because you have learned how to manage your habits. Having mastered one problem, you approach other problems with more confidence. You undertake new tasks with more assurance. Confidence begets confidence; success begets success.

It's a fine, new world that awaits the ex-smoker, full of enjoyment and pleasure. He has five wonderful freedoms—freedom from illness, freedom from annoyance, freedom from fatigue, freedom for full enjoyment of life with all five senses, and freedom for future achievements. He's really living!

2. How Not To Proceed

As you spread the word that you are going to stop smoking, people will rush in with helpful advice. It usually begins, "I had a friend who stopped smoking and *he* . . ." It rarely begins, "I stopped smoking, and *I* . . ." Information about what John's sister's Aunt Myra's cousin did, won't do you any good. Such ineffectual systems are built upon idle talk instead of sound psychological method.

Before considering the right way to proceed in breaking the smoking habit, we'll look at some of the pitfalls. Don't take drugs; they are either dangerous or useless. Just as undependable is the idea of substituting a pipe for cigarettes, or vice versa, because you're still subjecting your system to the attacks of a tobacco product. Not buying your own cigarettes and counting on shame to keep you from smoking other people's, is a system that never works.

Don't bet that you will stop smoking and expect the loss of money to keep you in line; that insures your taking up the habit again as soon as the bet is over. Rationing your cigarettes or cutting them down gradually, makes them more important. Dr. Link's system (to be described later) suggests you spend 6 months breaking down the habit of smoking, but it is a difficult and impractical solution for the average human being.

Don't try these systems. They've been tested by smokers and they do not work!

DON'T DEPEND ON DRUGS AND SUBSTITUTES

The worst scheme of all is the use of some kind of drug. Neither dangerous drugs nor taste-destroying analgesics can stop you from smoking. The reasons why they won't work have been explained at the beginning of the book.

Almost as bad is the substitution of a pipe for cigarettes or cigars. The end result of this substitution is usually annoyance. The heavy smokers soon return to their old ways. A friend of mine who tried this idea finished up smoking both a pipe and cigars. Sometimes the smoker switches permanently from cigarettes to a pipe, which still feeds his habit and his system with nicotine and tobacco tars. In the case of women, such a substitution is inapplicable. Obviously, most women won't smoke pipes even if they want to stop smoking cigarettes.

In a poll of ex-smokers, nobody ever succeeded in breaking the habit by substituting a pipe. Using the substitution method and failing, adds the weight of failure to the fear that the habit cannot be broken. This makes it more difficult to try again, although that's exactly what should be done. The use of any tobacco products at all is bad for you. Why not make a clean break?

DON'T TRY TO STOP SMOKING—BY SMOKING OTHERS' CIGARETTES

One fine day you decide smoking is bad for you. "I won't buy any more cigarettes," you proclaim. "If it gets to the point where I can't stand it, I'll chisel a smoke. Smoking other people's cigarettes, I won't have the gall to ask for too many. Eventually, I'll just cut it out altogether."

This is a beautiful system for killing your own self-respect. You are afraid to say you are going to stop smoking altogether. It's like admitting you don't trust yourself. Actually you haven't given yourself half a chance; you *can* stop if you do it properly. Why depend upon an artificial deterrent instead of your own desire to keep you from smoking? A vague idea of stopping sometime in the future is too hazy and indefinite to do any good.

In the end you stand before the tobacco counter where you feebly ask for a pack of your usual brand. You have reached the point where shame stopped you from smoking more of other people's cigarettes. But, it hasn't killed your desire to smoke. It's done nothing at all to break your habit pattern of smoking. It has even made you more conscious of your desire to smoke. This was exactly what happened to me 15 years ago when I tried the method. Don't try to shame yourself out of smoking—it won't work.

BIG MONEY-BET PENALTIES ARE A BLIND ALLEY

One of the weirder ways for breaking the smoking habit is the money-bet system. The man who touted this sat down and wrote a book about his experiences. He swore by the system and boasted that it enabled him to stop smoking. However, he resumed his cigarettes when the bet was over—which means the system didn't work.

Briefly, this was his idea. He bet a large sum of money, equal to 6 months' rent, that he could stop smoking for 6 months. He won the bet and claimed that it was only the thought of losing such a large sum of money which kept him from smoking. The glaring defect in his plan shows up in his last chapter. There, he describes how conscious he is that the 6-month period is coming to a close. He is waiting feverishly for the hour when he will be able to smoke a cigarette. He even sets his alarm to ring at the exact moment when the time will be up, to notify him of the earliest second when he can take a puff!

His plan is based on the fear of losing a large sum of money. He gives no thought at all to the need for breaking the habit pattern which made him smoke. He is conscious of wanting to smoke the whole time the bet is on; his system makes him more conscious and more desirous of smoking—not less so.

In addition, there are few of us who could scrape up a sum sizable enough to frighten us into winning such a gamble. Betting you can stop smoking for a certain period of time tests your will power, and measures the value money has for you. It doesn't help you break the cigarette habit. The moment you place a limit on the time you will not smoke, you defeat yourself. Saying you won't smoke for 6 months or 6 years is tantamount to saying you are not going to give up smoking.

RATIONING CIGARETTES MAKES SMOKING MORE IMPORTANT

Another self-defeating system, on a smaller scale, is rationing. To declare you are going to stop smoking by rationing your cigarettes is to blow up the importance of the rationed cigarettes. They seem more desirable than ever before.

You decide to smoke one cigarette an hour. For the first 10 minutes, you feel good. When 15 minutes have passed, you look at the clock and muse on how slowly the hands are moving. At the half-hour mark, you look up again. All you can think of is the way that cigarette is going to taste at the end of the hour. The appointed time rolls around and you light up with frenzied eagerness.

Under the rationing system, you spend your whole day watching the clock and longing for the times when you permit yourself to smoke. You have never thought about smoking as much as now. Inevitably, a minor crisis arises. Something upsets you and you reach for a cigarette automatically, breaking your system into little pieces. Soon you are back to smoking at your old rate.

There's a variation of the rationing method. You don't start smoking until a certain hour. You ration time instead of cigarettes. Perhaps you decide on noon. Your morning is filled with thoughts of the first cigarette, the rest of your day is filled with a blue, smoky haze.

After you have suffered under this system for a week, you realize you are smoking as much as you ever did. The difference is that you are now smoking more cigarettes per hour in the time you have allowed yourself to smoke. Deciding the system won't work, you go back to your old smoking habits. However, you've shortened the time between cigarettes and you'll probably smoke more than you ever did.

Wistfully, you decide that you'll never be able to give up smoking. That's true. You'll never, never do it if you use the rationing method.

PROFESSOR LINK'S SYSTEM TAKES TOO LONG

There is one method based on the fact that smoking is a habit—Dr. Henry Link's system. It calls upon you to follow a long, laborious process of habit breaking. It takes 6 months before you arrive at the point where you even think about giving up smoking.

You begin by interfering with your regular smoking habits. For example, suppose you are accustomed to placing your cigarettes on a table within easy reach for your evening's smoking. Under Link's method, you put your pack in another room so you will break the regular routine of reaching beside you for a cigarette. Instead, you will have to get up and walk into another room before you can smoke. This is to serve as a reminder that you are going to give up smoking.

You break up your automatic lighting of a cigarette by drawing one from your pack and leaving it beside you, unlit. Or, you do light it up and immediately snuff it out. Teasing yourself, and playing games like this, is more likely to underline the desirability of each cigarette you smoke. Just because smoking is a habit, you are likely to forget all the elaborate preparations you must go through before you can smoke. Sooner or later, you find yourself lighting up a cigarette in the old, automatic way.

Spending 6 months thinking how you can vary your smoking routine is too painful and difficult for the ordinary human being. There is no need to subject yourself to such a slow, uncertain, and inefficient method. You can stop smoking, it won't take 6 months, and you don't need an iron will.

3. You Are Ready To Begin

You have made progress without realizing it. You don't want to smoke, and you've decided to stop. This is the halfway mark! Using the right method to break the habit of smoking will take you sailing through the first, difficult days.

NO EXCEPTIONS

Now is the time to set the date. S-Day—this is the day when you are going to stop smoking completely and absolutely. Not for 6 months, or a year or 10 years, but *forever!*

Psychologists tell you to try for a goal you can achieve. You are about to do something you want very much to do, to stop smoking! Because you're convinced smoking is bad for you, you *can* stop!

Breaking the habit is nine-tenths conviction and one-tenth

method. Don't put the date, S-Day, way ahead in the future. Start with a bang while your resolution is still strong. You are never going to smoke again.

SET THE DATE IN THE NEAR FUTURE

There are several ways of choosing the date to make it easier for yourself. Set S-Day at a time when there is going to be a break in your usual routine. A weekend, which is a change from your workaday world, is a good time to begin; if it's a long weekend—so much the better. If you have a vacation scheduled in the next 4 weeks, the first day is excellent for putting your plan into action.

Strange as it may seem, another fine time to start is when you're laid up with a cold. (Don't wait for a cold to develop, however. Use it only if it comes along within the next 4 weeks.) If you're going into the hospital for an operation within a month from now, set this time to swear off smoking. Going off on a trip—that's a good time to start!

The important thing is to pick a date when your ordinary routine is changed. However, under no circumstances, use this requirement as an excuse for a long delay. Because you may be reading this book in the spring doesn't mean you can wait for your summer vacation before you set S-Day. It must be within the next month.

S-Day is not dependent on the moment when your smoking supplies are exhausted. Don't kid yourself by saying you will stop smoking when you have no more cigarettes left. S-Day is a definite date. In the next chapter, you'll find out what to do if you have any supplies left on S-Day.

ANTICIPATE YOUR PROBLEMS

If you know what to expect, you'll be able to meet the problems that arise. Arm yourself beforehand with a knowledge of how you'll feel when you first stop smoking. There will be problems to overcome. There'll be some tough moments, but not half as tough as you think.

Nobody ever died, nobody ever got sick because he was deprived of tobacco. All you have to do is follow the method outlined and you'll be a new person.

VARY YOUR ROUTINE

Don't forget that you are breaking a habit. Habits are reflexes which respond to certain stimuli. The habit pattern that led you to smoke in the past will still be operating, even though you have stopped responding to it by smoking. For this reason, don't carry cigarettes around with you after you stop smoking. You might find yourself lighting up automatically, without any intention of doing so.

Stimuli which made you smoke in the past, are still present in your day-to-day living. You will still respond to those stimuli by feeling a desire to smoke. Recognize the urges as part of an old habit pattern which you are breaking. Never give in to them!

For example—you have always associated coffee and cigarettes. Break the reflex chain by leaving the table and sitting elsewhere as soon as you have drunk your coffee. If it was your habit to light up a cigarette and sit down with the paper as soon as you got home from work, break the pattern— do something else when you first come home. Nibble on some food, on a cracker, or take a glass of tomato juice as you read the evening news.

You are calling the shots now. You can laugh at the tyranny of a habit which has made you dance for so many years.

You're ready to begin. You know there must be no exceptions. You have set the date, S-Day, for some time within the next month. Anticipate your problems and they won't get you down. Meet them by varying your routine. It won't be nearly as tough as you think. As long as you know the right way to proceed, you can be successful. You will break the smoking habit.

4. Ten Signposts to a Smokeless World

The right way of breaking the smoking habit is the easiest way. There are 10 simple rules to follow.

1. YOU MUST BE CONVINCED

The first step calls for a review of your ideas and attitudes on smoking. Have you a strong personal conviction that smoking is very bad for you, medically speaking? Do you understand why? If all the facts on smoking are not perfectly clear, go back and re-read the medical section of this book.

You cannot afford to view the effects of smoking halfheartedly. You must not attempt the following steps until you are sure you know exactly why smoking undermines your health and destroys your body. When the medical facts are fixed in your mind, you are ready to proceed.

2. ANNOUNCE YOU ARE GOING TO QUIT

Make the announcement to your family, friends, and coworkers that you are going to stop smoking; you'll see how interested they are. This is one subject about which everybody is curious. Surprisingly, you'll find people more eager to discuss smoking than politics or sex. There are so many people who want to give up smoking but don't know how, you'll be overwhelmed with questions.

When you make the announcement, some people will look on you as a hero, others will tell you it's impossible. Don't let anyone scare you. You'll succeed. Let everybody hear the medical reasons that made you decide. Explain the things you have learned by reading this book. Take them through the same processes you followed in reaching your decision.

You certainly owe it to your friends and loved ones to convince them to stop smoking. You don't want smoking to damage their lives any more than your own. In discussing the subject with them, you'll be helping yourself too.

3. FIND A PARTNER, IF POSSIBLE

Now find a partner. See whether you can convince someone in your family, or a friend whom you see frequently, or one of your co-workers, to go along with you. Choosing someone you see often is important. If two of you decide to stop smoking at the same time, it will be much easier for both. However, don't be discouraged if you cannot find someone to go along with you. Follow the procedure outlined and you will be able to stop smoking on your own.

There's an even more important reason for finding a partner than the mutual help you can give each other. You know the havoc smoking wreaks on your body. How can you let people you love suffer those dangers? How can you sit and watch your friends smoking their lives away?

If I had known earlier about the dangers of smoking, and been able to convince my wife, I might have prevented her heart attack. In finding a partner, you may save the health or life of someone close to you.

4. LIST YOUR 10 STRONGEST REASONS

If you haven't completed the list of what you personally dislike about smoking, sit down and do it right now. Put the list on a little card which will fit into your wallet or purse, so that you can carry it around with you all the time.

Originally, I listed 19 reasons why I detested smoking, but I boiled them down to 10 big ones. This is the way my list ran:

What I Hate About Smoking

1. Mouth always tastes terrible
2. Keeps me from sleeping
3. I'm a slave to the habit
4. Cuts my wind and endurance
5. Catch cold very easily
6. Can't stop coughing, throat raw
7. Heart, chest and back pains
8. Don't enjoy taste of cigarettes
9. Burns holes in my favorite suits
10. ALMOST KILLED MY WIFE!
    COULD KILL ME!

While you are thinking about it, write down all the reasons that occur to you. Then pick out the most objectionable 10 features of smoking and make out your list.

Carry the list around with you everywhere. Read it at night, the last thing before you go to sleep. Take it up in the morning and look at it. If you are waiting for somebody, pull out the list and glance over your reasons.

While reading your list, keep in mind how wonderful and free you will feel once you've stopped smoking. This goal of energy, pleasure, increased enjoyment of life, and freedom from disease is what you are striving for. This is a goal you can achieve because you want to stop smoking for good, sound reasons.

5. GET RID OF ALL SUPPLIES BY S-DAY

The evening before S-Day, assemble all your cigarettes or other smoking supplies. Smoke as many as you can, one after another. Try the exhaustion method. As you sit there chain-smoking, tell yourself this is what you have been holding on to. This is the habit from which you are freeing yourself. You will hate the sight of those cigarettes before you are finished. You'll end up saying to yourself, "Thank heavens I'm getting rid of this habit!"

Be sure you don't make yourself sick, however. When you feel as though you couldn't look at another cigarette, smoke just one more and stop. Don't try to smoke every last one. If smoking bothers you too much, don't try this method at all. Wait for the next morning when you will destroy what remains of your supplies publicly.

You wake up the next morning. It's S-Day! Get out of bed right away. You've already told everybody you're not smoking from this day forward. Get dressed quickly and then have a real good breakfast.

Publicly destroy all your remaining tobacco supplies today. This is a must! Have other people watch you doing it—your family, or friends. Inform anyone who doesn't know yet that you've given up smoking completely. Of course, you won't object to others' smoking. But tell people *you've* given up smoking, and why, when you're offered a cigarette. It goes without saying that you will refuse.

6. CIGARETTE SUSTITUTES FOR THE FIRST DAYS

You have been accustomed to sticking a cigarette into your mouth with frightening regularity. What to do with your mouth may bother you in the beginning. For the first days be prepared with hard candy, mints, chewing gum, nuts, or something pleasant to nibble on.

You don't have to worry about putting on weight. The need for substitutes will disappear. As a matter of fact, the substitute piece of candy or chewing gum will be an annoyance after a while.

Realize that this desire to draw on a cigarette is a desire to do something with the mouth. It is the outgrowth of a habit which goes back to babyhood. Something bothers baby and he pops his thumb in his mouth, or he sucks on a pacifier. While it helps to soothe baby, this system can't bring any real satisfaction to an adult. It's a hangover from babyhood, the baby's way of obtaining satisfaction.

Now that you are an adult, let your pleasures and satisfactions be adult. If a hangover from babyhood is translated into something harmful, like the cigarette habit, then it is certainly time for a change. Whether the new habit be chewing on a pencil, eating peanuts, or soothing yourself with cough drops or hard candies—any such substitute can take the place of smoking, and will help you tremendously.

7. OCCUPY YOUR HANDS

You will also wonder what to do with your hands in the beginning. Keep them busy. Fiddle with an object if you want to. It's perfectly safe to use substitute activities, like twirling a key chain, or doodling, or playing with a pencil, until the smoking habit is broken. Some people find it helps to carry around an *empty* cigarette holder for the first week. Don't worry about the substitute activities becoming habits; you won't need them long enough.

Also begin to use your hands when you speak. This is not a call for wild gestures, but for the subtle turn of a wrist that underlines a phrase, or the movement that gives color to a description. Hands are an interesting part of the individual. They express character and personality. When you are not using your hands, you'll eventually learn to relax them. This is a manifestation of poise and maturity the smoker never achieves.

8. BREATHE DEEPLY TO RELIEVE TENSION

Comes a moment when an overpowering urge for a smoke hits you. Stop whatever you are doing and take a deep, deep breath. Release the breath slowly, exhaling it through slightly parted lips. The change in your breathing pattern relaxes you.

If you can go to an open window and get fresh air into your lungs, so much the better. When you were a smoker, the deep breath you took occasionally was the only good you got out of smoking. Now you can put deep breathing to much better use.

9. REVIEW YOUR SUCCESS AND REWARD YOURSELF FOR IT

When you are tempted to smoke, think of how well you have succeeded up to this very moment. Count the hours—and later the days—you have gone without smoking. If an hour, surely you can double the time; if 2 hours, you can make it 4. If you've gone for a day or more without smoking, you can continue. As time goes on, you'll feel better and better. You will have a sense of exhilaration you never knew.

At the end of each day, reward yourself for your triumph. Indulge yourself in something special. You can afford little luxuries now you don't smoke. In the evening be good to yourself. Do something you particularly enjoy. You really deserve it.

The first evening, decide how you are going to reward yourself on the following day. You're entitled to pamper yourself while getting over the hump. After you've broken the back of the habit, you won't need these extra indulgences.

For a week or so, plan to do only those things you take pleasure in, to help you break the habit. This is very important!

A word of caution on your first smokeless week! Don't use this period to do something you dislike. It's not the time to make out your income tax, or go on a diet, or start the odd jobs around the house which you really don't want to do. The first week is the hardest, but it can be lots of fun.

10. NO EXCEPTIONS TO THE 'NO SMOKING' RULE

I'd like to write the last rule in letters 2 feet high. DO NOT MAKE A SINGLE EXCEPTION! DO NOT SMOKE A SINGLE CIGARETTE! DO NOT TAKE A SINGLE PUFF! You must not consider smoking ever again.

You must never go back to smoking any more than the re-formed alcoholic must go back to drinking. But what's so terrible about that? You have given up smoking for good. You are free, and it's wonderful.

And, if you fail, what do you do? Throw your hands up in disgust and hopelessness, calling yourself all kinds of names? Absolutely not! It isn't a matter of weak or strong will power. You have made a mistake in the learning process. Mistakes will happen. Don't give up. Go ahead.

Continue with your program. Review the medical effects of smoking and re-read this chapter. Then proceed as if the mistake had not happened.

As an additional aid, write out the rules for constant reference. Take the card on which you listed your reasons for disliking smoking. On the reverse side, write down the 10 sign-posts to the non-smoking world. Carry this card around with you everywhere.

Refer to it often during the first week. When a craving stirs in the solar plexus, take out the card and read it over. You have listed the reasons why smoking is so disagreeable to you; here is the list of rules for the other side of the card.

1. When you have a clear, medical conviction against smoking, you are ready to begin—not before.
2. Announce the day. "I stop smoking on ____(date)____."
3. Find a partner.
4. Tell everyone why smoking is no good, and try to convince others not to smoke.
5. Publicly destroy all supplies on S-Day.
6. Use substitutes for smoking as long as necessary.
7. Occupy your hands.
8. Breathe deeply if you become tense.
9. Review your success nightly and reward yourself for being good.
10. NO EXCEPTIONS!

Tomorrow will be easier, and each day thereafter. You have your future in the palm of your hand. Go ahead. Break the smoking habit and win your freedom!

5. Your First Smokeless Week

The first week is the hardest! You will be jittery; but the rewards of not smoking are so satisfying, it's worth the effort you put forth. Although breaking the habit is difficult in the beginning, it's never as tough as you think it's going to be.

As a matter of fact, the first day gives you a real taste of success. After that, the temptations spring up, but along with them you begin to enjoy your first freedom from the annoyances of smoking. By the end of the week, you know it isn't as hard as it seemed. You've licked the habit.

THE FIRST TASTE OF SUCCESS

The first day you are carried along by a feeling of accomplishment. The excitement of knowing you haven't smoked for 2 hours makes you feel you can double it. When you've gone half a day without smoking, you're as proud as the Englishman who conquered Mt. Everest. In the evening, you're surrounded with a warm aura of satisfaction because you've gone a whole day without smoking—for the first time in years and years. You go to sleep with a real sense of achievement.

GUARD AGAINST TEMPTATION

The second and third days are the toughest parts of the week for most people. By now, the tension mounts a little. You can take it, but you have to grit your teeth somewhat. Maybe you're irritable. You study the card a little harder. But over and above the discomfort, your pride is growing. You really begin to see that it can be done.

You are careful to keep supplied with candy or gum or whatever substitute you have chosen; and you will use it frequently if you are wise. These are the days when the public announcement that you have stopped smoking pays off. The little devils of temptation can't touch you when you think of how far and wide you broadcast your intention. Console yourself with the thought that this is the toughest time and you haven't smoked up till now. If you've been able to hold out so long, you'll be able to make it.

YOUR FIRST FREEDOM FROM ANNOYANCES OF SMOKING

Now you can start watching for the departure of those annoyances which used to plague you. Your cigarette cough is on the way out. Going, too, is that annoying post-nasal drip. You've scrubbed the nicotine stain off your fingers. No more yellow, discolored hands!

This is the time to visit your dentist and have him clean your teeth. You have done away with unpleasant-looking, tobacco-stained teeth. After you leave the dentist, your mouth feels wonderfully clean and fresh. The stale tobacco taste is gone forever.

IT ISN'T AS HARD AS YOU THOUGHT

Along about the fourth or fifth day, you're startled to realize you're over the hump. You've gone for considerable periods of time without even thinking about smoking. You are finding new energy and a new sense of well-being.

Don't keep it a secret. Let your friends know. More than likely, they'll ask you how you're doing before you have a chance to tell them. Most people's wistful desire to stop smoking will make them very curious about your progress. Tell them how it has been.

At the end of the first week, read the chapter on the fine, free world which awaits ex-smokers. Check off the pleasures you have experienced and those which await you. Tell others all about your first week.

Broadcast the fact that you haven't smoked for a week. Others are so anxious to know that it can be done; your success will give them courage. Describe your sense of achievement on the first smokeless day. Don't try to hide the temptations assailing you, but show also the beginnings of your liberation from the annoyances of smoking.

The first week is over. You've done it! You've got it licked! You've broken the smoking habit.

6. . . . and Thereafter

You have survived your first smokeless week with flying colors. Don't worry about the fleeting desire for a cigarette; it's natural. When it happens, you know what to do. But remember, you must never, never smoke again. When the first week is over, organize an Ex-Smokers' Club if you can. And keep trying to convince other people to stop smoking, for their sake and yours. Public commitment will keep you from backsliding.

FLEETING DESIRE TO SMOKE IS NATURAL

The end of the first smokeless week is a turning point. It's like going from courtship into marriage. The first 7 days correspond to the courtship. There are ups and downs, depression and elation. But always there is the knowledge you are working toward your goal. Then the girl says "Yes," and marriage lies ahead.

All of a sudden, your aim has been achieved and you are attacked by an awful feeling of uncertainty. Thoughts rise to plague you. There are moments you'd rather not get married. Isn't that a bad sign? Doesn't it mean the marriage won't work?

The same kind of uncertainty may attack you at the start of your second smokeless week or a little later. "I've gone all this time without smoking," you say. "Why should I still feel momentary urges to smoke?"

You begin to fear that the successful, first smokeless week is not going to give you all you want. "I'm not completely rid of the desire to smoke. Isn't that a bad sign? Doesn't that mean I would like to go on smoking?" Not at all! The fact that you haven't smoked for a week—or a month—is very good proof that you have broken the stranglehold of the smoking habit. Your drive to stop smoking has been a success. You don't really want to smoke again.

The groom's fleeting desire for his single state doesn't mean his marriage will be a failure. Your fleeting desire for a smoke doesn't mean that you have failed. In either case, it's a natural human reaction. This momentary period of self-doubt won't stop the bridegroom from being happy in his marriage, any more than it will stop the ex-smoker from being happy in his smokeless world. It doesn't mean that the ex-smoker can't be successful. After you've gotten through the first 7 days, you can live the rest of your life without smoking.

DON'T PLAY WITH FIRE! NEVER SMOKE AGAIN

You have broken an established habit, but it will take a long time for the habit to die completely. Eventually, however, disuse will destroy it. It's a slow procedure, but every smokeless day becomes easier to face.

You must never smoke again, not a single puff. Your memory of smoking is the most deceitful thing in the world. You have no idea how distasteful smoking will be to you now. Trying to smoke again will make you as sick as it did the very first time. The cigarette will taste like a combination of burnt rags and cow dung. Your system is now completely unaccustomed to nicotine.

Trying a cigarette to reinforce your dislike of smoking is a very dangerous procedure. The ex-nicotine addict cannot risk reassembling the old chain of stimuli and reflex habits which bound him when he was a smoker. Disuse has made your habit pattern inactive; it will stay inactive only so long as you do not go back to the drug which established it.

Don't deceive yourself by considering smoking at some future date—in moderation. The ex-smoker is like the ex-alcoholic. The ex-smoker can no more go back to smoking a little than the ex-alcoholic can go back to drinking a little. In either case, the little becomes a lot very quickly. It is so easy to re-establish old habit patterns, that one cigarette could undo the good work of months or even years.

ORGANIZE AN EX-SMOKERS' CLUB

There are various things you can do to keep from backsliding. For the early months, form a 90-Day Club of ex-smokers. It is helpful and reassuring to have other ex-smokers around you. You can understand each other's feelings and problems. You all have the same goal.

When you meet, discuss your fears and your weaknesses frankly. Comparison of experiences and problems will enable you to help one another. If you fear something will happen to make you start smoking again, talk it out with the others. Together you can achieve much that is difficult to do alone. Whether the club has 2 members or 10, it can aid you tremendously in the early days.

CONTINUE EFFORTS TO CONVINCE OTHERS TO STOP SMOKING

Keep on trying to convince your friends to stop smoking, not only for their sake but for your own. Talking to them about the effects of tobacco reinforces your own determination to stay away from it forever.

Furthermore, why let others suffer from the harm tobacco can do? Why keep your friends and family in the dark? Don't they deserve the protection of life and health your knowledge can give them?

WHAT TO DO ABOUT UNEXPECTED CRAVINGS, LATER ON

If a sudden desire to smoke takes you unawares, review the rules you used during your first week. Re-read the list of reasons why you disliked smoking so much. Figure out the amount of time you have gone without smoking. Realize that you will not go on experiencing moments of temptation like this much longer.

How long have you now gone without smoking? Divide that time in half. This will tell you approximately how long you may still be plagued with occasional cravings for a cigarette. They will occur less and less frequently.

If you follow the procedure outlined in this book, you will reach a point where you won't have the slightest desire for a cigarette ever again.

Congratulations, and healthy, happy living!

A PERSONAL WORD FROM MELVIN POWERS
PUBLISHER, WILSHIRE BOOK COMPANY

Dear Friend:

My goal is to publish interesting, informative, and inspirational books. You can help me accomplish this by answering the following questions, either by phone or by mail. Or, if convenient for you, I would welcome the opportunity to visit with you in my office and hear your comments in person.

Did you enjoy reading this book? Why?

Would you enjoy reading another similar book?

What idea in the book impressed you the most?

If applicable to your situation, have you incorporated this idea in your daily life?

Is there a chapter that could serve as a theme for an entire book? Please explain.

If you have an idea for a book, I would welcome discussing it with you. If you already have one in progress, write or call me concerning possible publication. I can be reached at (213) 875-1711 or (818) 983-1105.

Sincerely yours,
MELVIN POWERS

12015 Sherman Road
North Hollywood, California 91605

MELVIN POWERS SELF-IMPROVEMENT LIBRARY

ASTROLOGY

_____ ASTROLOGY: HOW TO CHART YOUR HOROSCOPE *Max Heindel*	5.00
_____ ASTROLOGY AND SEXUAL ANALYSIS *Morris C. Goodman*	5.00
_____ ASTROLOGY MADE EASY *Astarte*	5.00
_____ ASTROLOGY, ROMANCE, YOU AND THE STARS *Anthony Norvell*	5.00
_____ MY WORLD OF ASTROLOGY *Sydney Omarr*	7.00
_____ THOUGHT DIAL *Sydney Omarr*	4.00
_____ WHAT THE STARS REVEAL ABOUT THE MEN IN YOUR LIFE *Thelma White*	3.00

BRIDGE

_____ BRIDGE BIDDING MADE EASY *Edwin B. Kantar*	10.00
_____ BRIDGE CONVENTIONS *Edwin B. Kantar*	7.00
_____ BRIDGE HUMOR *Edwin B. Kantar*	5.00
_____ COMPETITIVE BIDDING IN MODERN BRIDGE *Edgar Kaplan*	7.00
_____ DEFENSIVE BRIDGE PLAY COMPLETE *Edwin B. Kantar*	15.00
_____ GAMESMAN BRIDGE—Play Better with Kantar *Edwin B. Kantar*	5.00
_____ HOW TO IMPROVE YOUR BRIDGE *Alfred Sheinwold*	5.00
_____ IMPROVING YOUR BIDDING SKILLS *Edwin B. Kantar*	4.00
_____ INTRODUCTION TO DECLARER'S PLAY *Edwin B. Kantar*	5.00
_____ INTRODUCTION TO DEFENDER'S PLAY *Edwin B. Kantar*	5.00
_____ KANTAR FOR THE DEFENSE *Edwin B. Kantar*	7.00
_____ KANTAR FOR THE DEFENSE VOLUME 2 *Edwin B. Kantar*	7.00
_____ SHORT CUT TO WINNING BRIDGE *Alfred Sheinwold*	3.00
_____ TEST YOUR BRIDGE PLAY *Edwin B. Kantar*	5.00
_____ VOLUME 2—TEST YOUR BRIDGE PLAY *Edwin B. Kantar*	5.00
_____ WINNING DECLARER PLAY *Dorothy Hayden Truscott*	7.00

BUSINESS, STUDY & REFERENCE

_____ CONVERSATION MADE EASY *Elliot Russell*	4.00
_____ EXAM SECRET *Dennis B. Jackson*	3.00
_____ FIX-IT BOOK *Arthur Symons*	2.00
_____ HOW TO DEVELOP A BETTER SPEAKING VOICE *M. Hellier*	4.00
_____ HOW TO SELF-PUBLISH YOUR BOOK & MAKE IT A BEST SELLER *Melvin Powers*	10.00
_____ INCREASE YOUR LEARNING POWER *Geoffrey A. Dudley*	3.00
_____ PRACTICAL GUIDE TO BETTER CONCENTRATION *Melvin Powers*	3.00
_____ PRACTICAL GUIDE TO PUBLIC SPEAKING *Maurice Forley*	5.00
_____ 7 DAYS TO FASTER READING *William S. Schaill*	5.00
_____ SONGWRITERS' RHYMING DICTIONARY *Jane Shaw Whitfield*	7.00
_____ SPELLING MADE EASY *Lester D. Basch & Dr. Milton Finkelstein*	3.00
_____ STUDENT'S GUIDE TO BETTER GRADES *J. A. Rickard*	3.00
_____ TEST YOURSELF—Find Your Hidden Talent *Jack Shafer*	3.00
_____ YOUR WILL & WHAT TO DO ABOUT IT *Attorney Samuel G. Kling*	5.00

CALLIGRAPHY

_____ ADVANCED CALLIGRAPHY *Katherine Jeffares*	7.00
_____ CALLIGRAPHER'S REFERENCE BOOK *Anne Leptich & Jacque Evans*	7.00
_____ CALLIGRAPHY—The Art of Beautiful Writing *Katherine Jeffares*	7.00
_____ CALLIGRAPHY FOR FUN & PROFIT *Anne Leptich & Jacque Evans*	7.00
_____ CALLIGRAPHY MADE EASY *Tina Serafini*	7.00

CHESS & CHECKERS

_____ BEGINNER'S GUIDE TO WINNING CHESS *Fred Reinfeld*	5.00
_____ CHESS IN TEN EASY LESSONS *Larry Evans*	5.00
_____ CHESS MADE EASY *Milton L. Hanauer*	3.00
_____ CHESS PROBLEMS FOR BEGINNERS *edited by Fred Reinfeld*	5.00
_____ CHESS SECRETS REVEALED *Fred Reinfeld*	2.00
_____ CHESS TACTICS FOR BEGINNERS *edited by Fred Reinfeld*	5.00
_____ CHESS THEORY & PRACTICE *Morry & Mitchell*	2.00
_____ HOW TO WIN AT CHECKERS *Fred Reinfeld*	3.00
_____ 1001 BRILLIANT WAYS TO CHECKMATE *Fred Reinfeld*	5.00
_____ 1001 WINNING CHESS SACRIFICES & COMBINATIONS *Fred Reinfeld*	5.00

_____ SOVIET CHESS *Edited by R. G. Wade*   3.00

COOKERY & HERBS

_____ CULPEPER'S HERBAL REMEDIES *Dr. Nicholas Culpeper*   3.00
_____ FAST GOURMET COOKBOOK *Poppy Cannon*   2.50
_____ GINSENG The Myth & The Truth *Joseph P. Hou*   3.00
_____ HEALING POWER OF HERBS *May Bethel*   4.00
_____ HEALING POWER OF NATURAL FOODS *May Bethel*   5.00
_____ HERB HANDBOOK *Dawn MacLeod*   3.00
_____ HERBS FOR HEALTH—How to Grow & Use Them *Louise Evans Doole*   4.00
_____ HOME GARDEN COOKBOOK—Delicious Natural Food Recipes *Ken Kraft*   3.00
_____ MEDICAL HERBALIST *edited by Dr. J. R. Yemm*   3.00
_____ VEGETABLE GARDENING FOR BEGINNERS *Hugh Wiberg*   2.00
_____ VEGETABLES FOR TODAY'S GARDENS *R. Milton Carleton*   2.00
_____ VEGETARIAN COOKERY *Janet Walker*   7.00
_____ VEGETARIAN COOKING MADE EASY & DELECTABLE *Veronica Vezza*   3.00
_____ VEGETARIAN DELIGHTS—A Happy Cookbook for Health *K. R. Mehta*   2.00
_____ VEGETARIAN GOURMET COOKBOOK *Joyce McKinnel*   3.00

GAMBLING & POKER

_____ ADVANCED POKER STRATEGY & WINNING PLAY *A. D. Livingston*   5.00
_____ HOW TO WIN AT DICE GAMES *Skip Frey*   3.00
_____ HOW TO WIN AT POKER *Terence Reese & Anthony T. Watkins*   5.00
_____ WINNING AT CRAPS *Dr. Lloyd T. Commins*   4.00
_____ WINNING AT GIN *Chester Wander & Cy Rice*   3.00
_____ WINNING AT POKER—An Expert's Guide *John Archer*   5.00
_____ WINNING AT 21—An Expert's Guide *John Archer*   5.00
_____ WINNING POKER SYSTEMS *Norman Zadeh*   3.00

HEALTH

_____ BEE POLLEN *Lynda Lyngheim & Jack Scagnetti*   3.00
_____ DR. LINDNER'S SPECIAL WEIGHT CONTROL METHOD *P. G. Lindner, M.D.*   2.00
_____ HELP YOURSELF TO BETTER SIGHT *Margaret Darst Corbett*   3.00
_____ HOW YOU CAN STOP SMOKING PERMANENTLY *Ernest Caldwell*   5.00
_____ MIND OVER PLATTER *Peter G. Lindner, M.D.*   3.00
_____ NATURE'S WAY TO NUTRITION & VIBRANT HEALTH *Robert J. Scrutton*   3.00
_____ NEW CARBOHYDRATE DIET COUNTER *Patti Lopez-Pereira*   2.00
_____ REFLEXOLOGY *Dr. Maybelle Segal*   4.00
_____ REFLEXOLOGY FOR GOOD HEALTH *Anna Kaye & Don C. Matchan*   5.00
_____ 30 DAYS TO BEAUTIFUL LEGS *Dr. Marc Selner*   3.00
_____ YOU CAN LEARN TO RELAX *Dr. Samuel Gutwirth*   3.00
_____ YOUR ALLERGY—What To Do About It *Allan Knight, M.D.*   3.00

HOBBIES

_____ BEACHCOMBING FOR BEGINNERS *Norman Hickin*   2.00
_____ BLACKSTONE'S MODERN CARD TRICKS *Harry Blackstone*   5.00
_____ BLACKSTONE'S SECRETS OF MAGIC *Harry Blackstone*   5.00
_____ COIN COLLECTING FOR BEGINNERS *Burton Hobson & Fred Reinfeld*   5.00
_____ ENTERTAINING WITH ESP *Tony 'Doc' Shiels*   2.00
_____ 400 FASCINATING MAGIC TRICKS YOU CAN DO *Howard Thurston*   5.00
_____ HOW I TURN JUNK INTO FUN AND PROFIT *Sari*   3.00
_____ HOW TO WRITE A HIT SONG & SELL IT *Tommy Boyce*   7.00
_____ JUGGLING MADE EASY *Rudolf Dittrich*   3.00
_____ MAGIC FOR ALL AGES *Walter Gibson*   4.00
_____ MAGIC MADE EASY *Byron Wels*   2.00
_____ STAMP COLLECTING FOR BEGINNERS *Burton Hobson*   3.00

HORSE PLAYERS' WINNING GUIDES

_____ BETTING HORSES TO WIN *Les Conklin*   5.00
_____ ELIMINATE THE LOSERS *Bob McKnight*   5.00
_____ HOW TO PICK WINNING HORSES *Bob McKnight*   5.00
_____ HOW TO WIN AT THE RACES *Sam (The Genius) Lewin*   5.00
_____ HOW YOU CAN BEAT THE RACES *Jack Kavanagh*   5.00

____ SEX WITHOUT GUILT *Albert Ellis, Ph.D.*		5.00
____ SEXUALLY ADEQUATE MALE *Frank S. Caprio, M.D.*		3.00
____ SEXUALLY FULFILLED MAN *Dr. Rachel Copelan*		5.00
____ STAYING IN LOVE *Dr. Norton F. Kristy*		7.00

MELVIN POWERS' MAIL ORDER LIBRARY

____ HOW TO GET RICH IN MAIL ORDER *Melvin Powers*		20.00
____ HOW TO WRITE A GOOD ADVERTISEMENT *Victor O. Schwab*		20.00
____ MAIL ORDER MADE EASY *J. Frank Brumbaugh*		20.00

METAPHYSICS & OCCULT

____ BOOK OF TALISMANS, AMULETS & ZODIACAL GEMS *William Pavitt*		7.00
____ CONCENTRATION—A Guide to Mental Mastery *Mouni Sadhu*		5.00
____ EXTRA-TERRESTRIAL INTELLIGENCE—The First Encounter		6.00
____ FORTUNE TELLING WITH CARDS *P. Foli*		5.00
____ HOW TO INTERPRET DREAMS, OMENS & FORTUNE TELLING SIGNS *Gettings*		5.00
____ HOW TO UNDERSTAND YOUR DREAMS *Geoffrey A. Dudley*		5.00
____ ILLUSTRATED YOGA *William Zorn*		3.00
____ IN DAYS OF GREAT PEACE *Mouni Sadhu*		3.00
____ LSD—THE AGE OF MIND *Bernard Roseman*		2.00
____ MAGICIAN—His Training and Work *W. E. Butler*		3.00
____ MEDITATION *Mouni Sadhu*		7.00
____ MODERN NUMEROLOGY *Morris C. Goodman*		5.00
____ NUMEROLOGY—ITS FACTS AND SECRETS *Ariel Yvon Taylor*		3.00
____ NUMEROLOGY MADE EASY *W. Mykian*		5.00
____ PALMISTRY MADE EASY *Fred Gettings*		5.00
____ PALMISTRY MADE PRACTICAL *Elizabeth Daniels Squire*		5.00
____ PALMISTRY SECRETS REVEALED *Henry Frith*		4.00
____ PROPHECY IN OUR TIME *Martin Ebon*		2.50
____ SUPERSTITION—Are You Superstitious? *Eric Maple*		2.00
____ TAROT *Mouni Sadhu*		10.00
____ TAROT OF THE BOHEMIANS *Papus*		7.00
____ WAYS TO SELF-REALIZATION *Mouni Sadhu*		7.00
____ WITCHCRAFT, MAGIC & OCCULTISM—A Fascinating History *W. B. Crow*		7.00
____ WITCHCRAFT—THE SIXTH SENSE *Justine Glass*		7.00
____ WORLD OF PSYCHIC RESEARCH *Hereward Carrington*		2.00

SELF-HELP & INSPIRATIONAL

____ CHARISMA How To Get "That Special Magic" *Marcia Grad*		7.00
____ DAILY POWER FOR JOYFUL LIVING *Dr. Donald Curtis*		5.00
____ DYNAMIC THINKING *Melvin Powers*		5.00
____ GREATEST POWER IN THE UNIVERSE *U. S. Andersen*		7.00
____ GROW RICH WHILE YOU SLEEP *Ben Sweetland*		7.00
____ GROWTH THROUGH REASON *Albert Ellis, Ph.D.*		7.00
____ GUIDE TO PERSONAL HAPPINESS *Albert Ellis, Ph.D. & Irving Becker, Ed. D.*		7.00
____ HANDWRITING ANALYSIS MADE EASY *John Marley*		5.00
____ HANDWRITING TELLS *Nadya Olyanova*		7.00
____ HELPING YOURSELF WITH APPLIED PSYCHOLOGY *R. Henderson*		2.00
____ HOW TO ATTRACT GOOD LUCK *A. H. Z. Carr*		7.00
____ HOW TO BE GREAT *Dr. Donald Curtis*		5.00
____ HOW TO DEVELOP A WINNING PERSONALITY *Martin Panzer*		5.00
____ HOW TO DEVELOP AN EXCEPTIONAL MEMORY *Young & Gibson*		5.00
____ HOW TO LIVE WITH A NEUROTIC *Albert Ellis, Ph. D.*		5.00
____ HOW TO OVERCOME YOUR FEARS *M. P. Leahy, M.D.*		3.00
____ HOW TO SUCCEED *Brian Adams*		7.00
____ HUMAN PROBLEMS & HOW TO SOLVE THEM *Dr. Donald Curtis*		5.00
____ I CAN *Ben Sweetland*		7.00
____ I WILL *Ben Sweetland*		3.00
____ KNIGHT IN THE RUSTY ARMOR *Robert Fisher*		10.00
____ LEFT-HANDED PEOPLE *Michael Barsley*		5.00
____ MAGIC IN YOUR MIND *U. S. Andersen*		7.00

____ MAGIC OF THINKING BIG *Dr. David J. Schwartz*		3.00
____ MAGIC OF THINKING SUCCESS *Dr. David J. Schwartz*		7.00
____ MAGIC POWER OF YOUR MIND *Walter M. Germain*		7.00
____ MENTAL POWER THROUGH SLEEP SUGGESTION *Melvin Powers*		3.00
____ NEVER UNDERESTIMATE THE SELLING POWER OF A WOMAN *Dottie Walters*		7.00
____ NEW GUIDE TO RATIONAL LIVING *Albert Ellis, Ph.D. & R. Harper, Ph.D.*		7.00
____ PROJECT YOU *A Manual of Rational Assertiveness Training Paris & Casey*		6.00
____ PSYCHO-CYBERNETICS *Maxwell Maltz, M.D.*		5.00
____ PSYCHOLOGY OF HANDWRITING *Nadya Olyanova*		7.00
____ SALES CYBERNETICS *Brian Adams*		7.00
____ SCIENCE OF MIND IN DAILY LIVING *Dr. Donald Curtis*		7.00
____ SECRET OF SECRETS *U. S. Andersen*		7.00
____ SECRET POWER OF THE PYRAMIDS *U. S. Andersen*		7.00
____ SELF-THERAPY FOR THE STUTTERER *Malcolm Frazer*		3.00
____ SUCCESS-CYBERNETICS *U. S. Andersen*		7.00
____ 10 DAYS TO A GREAT NEW LIFE *William E. Edwards*		3.00
____ THINK AND GROW RICH *Napoleon Hill*		7.00
____ THINK YOUR WAY TO SUCCESS *Dr. Lew Losoncy*		5.00
____ THREE MAGIC WORDS *U. S. Andersen*		7.00
____ TREASURY OF COMFORT *edited by Rabbi Sidney Greenberg*		5.00
____ TREASURY OF THE ART OF LIVING *Sidney S. Greenberg*		5.00
____ WHAT YOUR HANDWRITING REVEALS *Albert E. Hughes*		3.00
____ YOUR SUBCONSCIOUS POWER *Charles M. Simmons*		7.00
____ YOUR THOUGHTS CAN CHANGE YOUR LIFE *Dr. Donald Curtis*		7.00

SPORTS

____ BICYCLING FOR FUN AND GOOD HEALTH *Kenneth E. Luther*		2.00
____ BILLIARDS—Pocket • Carom • Three Cushion *Clive Cottingham, Jr.*		5.00
____ CAMPING-OUT 101 Ideas & Activities *Bruno Knobel*		2.00
____ COMPLETE GUIDE TO FISHING *Vlad Evanoff*		2.00
____ HOW TO IMPROVE YOUR RACQUETBALL *Lubarsky Kaufman & Scagnetti*		5.00
____ HOW TO WIN AT POCKET BILLIARDS *Edward D. Knuchell*		5.00
____ JOY OF WALKING *Jack Scagnetti*		3.00
____ LEARNING & TEACHING SOCCER SKILLS *Eric Worthington*		3.00
____ MOTORCYCLING FOR BEGINNERS *I. G. Edmonds*		3.00
____ RACQUETBALL FOR WOMEN *Toni Hudson, Jack Scagnetti & Vince Rondone*		3.00
____ RACQUETBALL MADE EASY *Steve Lubarsky, Rod Delson & Jack Scagnetti*		5.00
____ SECRET OF BOWLING STRIKES *Dawson Taylor*		5.00
____ SECRET OF PERFECT PUTTING *Horton Smith & Dawson Taylor*		5.00
____ SOCCER—The Game & How to Play It *Gary Rosenthal*		5.00
____ STARTING SOCCER *Edward F. Dolan, Jr.*		5.00

TENNIS LOVERS' LIBRARY

____ BEGINNER'S GUIDE TO WINNING TENNIS *Helen Hull Jacobs*		2.00
____ HOW TO IMPROVE YOUR TENNIS—Style, Strategy & Analysis *C. Wilson*		2.00
____ PSYCH YOURSELF TO BETTER TENNIS *Dr. Walter A. Luszki*		2.00
____ TENNIS FOR BEGINNERS, *Dr. H. A. Murray*		2.00
____ TENNIS MADE EASY *Joel Brecheen*		4.00
____ WEEKEND TENNIS—How to Have Fun & Win at the Same Time *Bill Talbert*		3.00
____ WINNING WITH PERCENTAGE TENNIS—Smart Strategy *Jack Lowe*		2.00

WILSHIRE PET LIBRARY

____ DOG OBEDIENCE TRAINING *Gust Kessopulos*		5.00
____ DOG TRAINING MADE EASY & FUN *John W. Kellogg*		3.00
____ HOW TO BRING UP YOUR PET DOG *Kurt Unkelbach*		2.00
____ HOW TO RAISE & TRAIN YOUR PUPPY *Jeff Griffen*		5.00

*The books listed above can be obtained from your book dealer or directly from
Melvin Powers. When ordering, please remit $1.00 postage for the first book
and 50¢ for each additional book.*

Melvin Powers

12015 Sherman Road, No. Hollywood, California 91605

HOW TO GET RICH IN MAIL ORDER
by Melvin Powers

Contents:

1. How to Develop Your Mail Order Expertise 2. How to Find a Unique Product or Service to Sell 3. How to Make Money with Classified Ads 4. How to Make Money with Display Ads 5. The Unlimited Potential for Making Money with Direct Mail 6. How to Copycat Successful Mail Order Operations 7. How I Created A Best Seller Using the Copycat Technique 8. How to Start and Run a Profitable Mail Order, Special Interest Book or Record Business 9. I Enjoy Selling Books by Mail—Some of My Successful and Not-So-Successful Ads and Direct Mail Circulars 10. Five of My Most Successful Direct Mail Pieces That Sold and Are Still Selling Millions of Dollars Worth of Books 11. Melvin Powers' Mail Order Success Strategy—Follow It and You'll Become a Millionaire 12. How to Sell Your Products to Mail Order Companies, Retail Outlets, Jobbers, and Fund Raisers for Maximum Distribution and Profits 13. How to Get Free Display Ads and Publicity That Can Put You on the Road to Riches 14. How to Make Your Advertising Copy Sizzle to Make You Wealthy 15. Questions and Answers to Help You Get Started Making Money in Your Own Mail Order Business 16. A Personal Word from Melvin Powers **8½" x 11" — 352 Pages . . . $21 postpaid**

HOW TO SELF-PUBLISH YOUR BOOK AND HAVE THE FUN AND EXCITEMENT OF BEING A BEST-SELLING AUTHOR
by Melvin Powers

An expert's step-by-step guide to marketing your book successfully

176 Pages . . . $11.00 postpaid

A NEW GUIDE TO RATIONAL LIVING
by Albert Ellis, Ph.D. & Robert A. Harper, Ph.D.

Contents:

1. How Far Can You Go With Self-Analysis? 2. You Feel the Way You Think 3. Feeling Well by Thinking Straight 4. How You Create Your Feelings 5. Thinking Yourself Out of Emotional Disturbances 6. Recognizing and Attacking Neurotic Behavior 7. Overcoming the Influences of the Past 8. Does Reason Always Prove Reasonable? 9. Refusing to Feel Desperately Unhappy 10. Tackling Dire Needs for Approval 11. Eradicating Dire Fears of Failure 12. How to Stop Blaming and Start Living 13. How to Feel Undepressed though Frustrated 14. Controlling Your Own Destiny 15. Conquering Anxiety

256 Pages . . . $7.50 postpaid

PSYCHO-CYBERNETICS
A New Technique for Using Your Subconscious Power
by Maxwell Maltz, M.D., F.I.C.S.

Contents:

1. The Self Image: Your Key to a Better Life 2. Discovering the Success Mechanism Within You 3. Imagination—The First Key to Your Success Mechanism 4. Dehypnotize Yourself from False Beliefs 5. How to Utilize the Power of Rational Thinking 6. Relax and Let Your Success Mechanism Work for You 7. You Can Acquire the Habit of Happiness 8. Ingredients of the Success-Type Personality and How to Acquire Them 9. The Failure Mechanism: How to Make It Work For You Instead of Against You 10. How to Remove Emotional Scars, or How to Give Yourself an Emotional Face Lift 11. How to Unlock Your Real Personality 12. Do-It-Yourself Tranquilizers **288 Pages . . . $5.50 postpaid**

A PRACTICAL GUIDE TO SELF-HYPNOSIS
by Melvin Powers

Contents:

1. What You Should Know About Self-Hypnosis 2. What About the Dangers of Hypnosis? 3. Is Hypnosis the Answer? 4. How Does Self-Hypnosis Work? 5. How to Arouse Yourself from the Self-Hypnotic State 6. How to Attain Self-Hypnosis 7. Deepening the Self-Hypnotic State 8. What You Should Know About Becoming an Excellent Subject 9. Techniques for Reaching the Somnambulistic State 10. A New Approach to Self-Hypnosis When All Else Fails 11. Psychological Aids and Their Function 12. The Nature of Hypnosis 13. Practical Applications of Self-Hypnosis **128 Pages . . . $3.50 postpaid**

The books listed above can be obtained from your book dealer or directly from Melvin Powers.

Melvin Powers
12015 Sherman Road, No. Hollywood, California 91605

Notes

Notes

Notes

Notes

Notes

Notes

Notes